JOKES

JOKES

Outrageous Bits, Atrocious Puns,
and Ridiculous Routines
for Those Who Love Jests

Paul Dickson

Illustrated by Don Addis

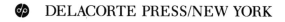 DELACORTE PRESS/NEW YORK

Published by
Delacorte Press
1 Dag Hammarskjold Plaza
New York, N.Y. 10017

Grateful acknowledgment is made for permission to
reprint excerpts from the following:

Glenn Collins collection of Chattanooga Choo Choo
jokes. © 1975 The New York Times Company.

Kansas City tourist tips by William Tammeus from
"Howdy Friend," *Kansas City Star-Times.*

"Do Its" from *Maledicta, the International Journal
of Verbal Aggression,* Volume 4, edited by Reinhold
Aman.

Cartoon by Don Addis on page 12 appears with
the permission of *The St. Petersburg Times.*

Manufactured in the United States of America

First printing

Library of Congress Cataloging in Publication Data
Dickson, Paul.
 Jokes.

 1. American wit and humor.   I. Addis, Don.
II. Title.
PN6162.D47   1984   818'.5402
ISBN 0-385-29333-X
Library of Congress Catalog Card Number: 83-17660

Dedicated to the scores of joke tellers and hoarders who let me borrow their best stuff.

They know who they are, but in case any of them try to squirm out of it, they are all listed at the back of the book. The author, of course, takes responsibility for all the good jokes while the clunkers should be blamed on those who so generously helped.

Contents

Preface   ix

Introduction   xi

  1. Flies in the Soup   1

  2. At the Pearly Gates   13

  3. The Lowest Form of the Lowest Form   24

  4. "Doc . . . Next"   34

  5. Punintended   37

  6. Too Much Saxon Violence   47

  7. The Chattanooga Challenge   51

  8. Here Come the Elephants   57

  9. Said Swiftly   64

 10. Operknockety Tunes   83

 11. Shaggy Dog Show   94

 12. The Willies   115

 13. Making Mary   122

 14. Punishments   125

 15. Many Hands Make Light Work   129

 16. Fort Knocks—The Master Collector   138

 17. The Voice from the Audience   149

 18. Tourist Tips   155

 19. Slurred Visions   159

20. Eternal Questions   174

21. Martians, Panhandlers, and
    a Few Cannibals   180

22. What's the Difference?   191

23. A School of Heard Knocks   196

24. Ménagerie à Trois   204

25. Personal Worst   214

26. Jokebooks and Magazines   226

27. Joke Museum Announced   232

28. But Seriously, Folks . . .   234

PREFACE

The main obligation is to amuse yourself.
—S. J. Perelman

I have always believed that one of the goals of a civilized life is putting together one's own joke collection. It is one of those few things one can do which require no justification or mindless blather about relevance. It is in the same class as whipping up the perfect omelette or hitting a home run in that anyone who could question the importance of such deeds is *ipso facto* irrelevant and out of touch with mortal realities. Despite years of trial and error I am still a flop as an omelette cook and, middle-age fantasies notwithstanding, I've never hit a home run; but as for the jokebook ... my time has come.

INTRODUCTION:

Funny Formula Jokes

Men show their character in nothing more clearly than what they think laughable.

— Alexander Pope

"Why does a chicken cross the road?"
"That wasn't no chicken — that was my wife."

— Bennett Cerf

You don't have to be a psychologist to realize that the jokes a person dotes on are a direct reflection of the person who tells them. My fascination has always been for those with a comfortable and immediately recognizable format: formula jokes. These are the jokes which lend themselves to endless variation starting with a basic theme or formula. Most of them are absurd to begin with and become more so as variation is piled on variation.

I believe that a fascination for this type of joke reveals the same kind of classical mentality which leads to a preference for sonnets over free verse, ballet over modern dance, and paper towels in public rest rooms over those damn air blowers. If this reveals a form of deep cultural conservatism, so be it.

Rather than getting bogged down in windy definitions, here are two admittedly subjective lists which quickly separate the joke universe into two major camps which I have cleverly termed "formula" and "other."

It is difficult to say exactly what goes into the making of a classic Column A personality, but deep self-analysis has led me to believe that in my own case there were five very important incidents and influences. Here they are in chronological order presented for the insight and uplift of others.

A. *Formula*	B. *Other*
Gleefully corny.	Sophisticated.
Funny.	Not so funny.
Very short or very long.	Longish.
Akin to early Woody Allen movies.	Akin to later Woody Allen films.
Kids love 'em.	Kids don't know what the hell you're talking about.
Can be dirty.	Can be sexually explicit.
Geared to getting guffaws and groans.	Pitched to polite laughter.
Typical opening: "Two poodles go into a bar and order martinis . . . ."	*Typical opening:* "Two human beings go into a bar and order white wine . . . ."
The kind of joke you'd tell W. C. Fields, Fred Allen, or Joan Rivers.	The kind of joke you'd tell Irving R. Levine, Dr. Joyce Brothers, or Ingmar Bergman.
Told by people who worried that when the U.S. recognized Red China, Taiwan would get back at us by cutting off the supply of whoopie cushions.	Told by people who fret about the incorrect use of the word "hopefully" and talk about dental flossing in public.
Helps identify the teller as a person of grace, wit, and style.	Does no such thing.

1. My father loved the most basic joke and riddle forms, and though he could be quite serious he was also the kind of man who thought, correctly, that it was right that his children have full command of the basic formulaic questions and their rich array of answers. "What's black and white and red all over?" he would ask and then come up with one of a dozen variant answers. It was also his belief that no child should ever visit our house without being asked, "What's the difference between an elephant and a mailbox?" Intimidated, the kids would always say they didn't know, which gave him the chance to reply, "I'd never send you to mail a letter."

After years of training, one morning I approached my father with the variant question:

"Who was that ladle I saw you with last night?"

He thought for a minute and said he didn't know.

I beamed and shot back, "That was no ladle, that was a spoon."

Not to belabor the obvious; but it was a proud moment for both of us.

2. Another early factor was the fact that I was born and brought up in Yonkers, New York, which ranks with Tickfaw, Louisiana, and Podunk, Massachusetts, as one of the most inherently funny names on the map of America. Unlike Tickfaw and Podunk, however, it was also loaded with funny people — Sid Caesar, Morey Amsterdam, Art Carney, were all born or lived there — and it was, along with Hoboken, the place that comedians used when they needed a place name for a gag and that songwriters used for tricky rhymes. ("We'll go to Yonkers, where true love conquers.") It rivaled Nantucket as a locale in limericks and it is the only place in America from which letters to "Dear Abby" can be signed "Bonkers in Yonkers." Coming from Yonkers could not actually make one funnier or a better joke teller, but it certainly helped and it was certainly not a handicap like coming from a euphoniously named place like Atlanta or Portland.

3. During the summers of 1959 and 1960 I worked for the Otis Elevator Company in Yonkers. I was in college at that time and each fall when I returned, my various professors would ask me what I had done during the summer. Almost without exception a variation on the following exchange took place:

Prof: "What did you do last summer?"

Me: "I worked for an elevator company."

Prof: (Long pause) "I'll bet that had its ups and downs."

This was then followed by studied professorial laughter, which, as anyone who has ever come within five miles of an institution of high learning knows, is generally unlike any other sound on earth.

The first few times this ritual took place I was vaguely irritated by the fact that these great teachers were so smug about a gag that had presumably been around since Elisha Graves Otis rigged his first elevator in New York City in 1852.

Then it dawned on me that this was giving these professors a great deal of pleasure and I began to understand that one of the great gifts you can offer another person is a tidy straight line. During my second summer at Otis I learned from other collegiate summer workers that they had participated in the same ritual.

Years later the importance of the elevator joke was brought home to me when I ran into one of my old professors on the streets of New York. Did he recall the brilliant if flawed papers I had handed him? No. What he remembered was the fact that I had worked in an elevator factory, and he then repeated *his* joke.*

---

*Over the years I've spoken with elevator operators about this and find that they are not only plagued with the ups-and-downs line but are also hit with "I'm sure you raised a number of fine families in your time" and "Could you let me off on five if that's not taking you out of your way." During a brief, ill-considered time in which I worked for a brokerage house I discovered a group who were unable to say "Otis Elevator" without saying, "I wish I'd gotten in on the ground floor with that one."

4. One night in 1963, while serving in the U.S. Navy, I consumed most of a bowl of highly seasoned soup. The man sitting next to me suddenly made a horrible noise, spat soup, and then bellowed, "This soup is full of flies." They were aphids, actually (or, as some people call them, plant lice) and were small enough to masquerade as large chunks of ground pepper.

Ever since then I have experienced a slight wave of nausea upon hearing jokes which begin with the line "Waiter, there's a fly in my soup!" Curiously, however, I have chosen to deal with my aphid trauma by putting together what I think may be the absolutely definitive collection of such jokes — an effort akin to that of getting back on a horse after you've been thrown — which is proudly exhibited in this book.

5. Finally, for reasons unclear I enjoy a strange affliction which visits me in times of stress. It is that when the going gets tough, my mind fills with a collection of quick, corny jokes which relate to the situation at hand. One example will suffice.

Whenever I have a physical exam and am about to suffer the particular probing which David Brenner calls the one which makes a person feel like a hand puppet, my mind fills with jokes. Once it was a series of convoluted puns ("No, thanks," she said, "I gave at the orifice"), another time it was limericks ("There once was a nearsighted proctologist . . ."), but the last time it was "Doc . . . Next" jokes. "Doc . . . Next" jokes? Glad you asked:

"Doc, I get this terrible pain in my back every time I bend over."

"Then don't bend over. Next!"

"Doc, nobody ever pays any attention to me."

"Next!"

Given the fact that I am a confirmed Column-A personality, it was only natural that when it came time for me to assemble my kind of jokebook it would dwell on all those things I loved most: Little Willie rhymes, shaggy dogs, light-bulb jokes, pearly-gates stories, elephants, and so many more of the great themes and formats.

After years of thinking about it, what prompted me to do it right *now* was my growing realization that jokes need protection just as a fine old building might require protection from the wrecker's ball.

As I see it, the threat being posed is the creeping Column-B solemnization and academization of American humor. All of this came to my attention a few years back when I got on some master mailing list which has brought me countless announcements for seminars and conferences on humor. I began reading papers and journal articles and even attended an international conference on the subject. The conclusion I reached was inescapable: humor in general and jokes in particular are becoming something to be probed and fretted over like some skin disease.

Sparing many of the more horrible details, here is what I found:

— Jargon-laden reports on the psychological and physiological aspects of humor are being delivered and published with stunning regularity. They carry titles like "Interfacing Vicarious Superiority and Interactive Incongruity Humor Theories" and "The Psycho-Social Bases of Scatological Humor: The Intra-Psychic Conflict between Autonomy and Conflict." Having heard some of these topics presented, I can assure you that their titles are often their most mirthful and comprehensible element. No aspect of humor is safe from the academic dragnet as jokes and wisecracks are coded and crammed into computers to help people get ready for humor conferences now being planned into the next century. One group has already picked the topics for its 1994 and 1995 conferences, which are, respectively, "Epiphany: The Humor of Sudden Insight," and

"Shibboleths: Humor for In-bonding and Out-bonding." Commenting on the phenomenon in *The New York Times* way back in 1973, Israel Shenker noted that things had already gotten to the point where "Tickling has generated a ponderous literature all its own. . . ."

— Human subjects have been hooked to electrodes, injected with chlorpromazine, given structured wittally tests, and even had their blood drawn and analyzed in the name of solving the "humor problem." In academic circles the word *problem* has been welded to the word *humor* whether it be in a paper like "The Problem of Humor in the Icelandic Family Sagas" (delivered at the Third International Conference on Humor in 1982) or in an assertion like "the shaggy dog story suggests many problems for folklorists" (made in the *Journal of American Folklore*).

— Some of the results of this research are astonishing. Jokes, for instance, have been turned into the most objectionable symbols among the post-Freudian psychologists and folkloric analysts. Elephant jokes have been tagged a possible subterfuge for white hostility and aggression against blacks (*Psychoanalytic Review*) and light-bulb jokes are seen as symbols of our sexual and political impotence (*Journal of American Folklore*). To read about jokes in the land which begat Dorothy Parker, Fred Allen, and Harry Hershfield is to read about neurosis, guilt, and despair.*

— Meanwhile, others are belaboring the most obvious points. One Ph.D., who obviously never heard a salesman use a few jokes to warm up a prospect, has discovered that jokes are sometimes used to influence

---

*The publication and ensuing popularity of the aptly titled *Truly Tasteless Jokes* by Blanche Knott will no doubt create no fewer than three symposia, a major conference, and ten journal articles. Before it is over it will be linked to the Spanish Inquisition, generalized primate anxiety, the Dow-Jones average, penis envy, and American apathy to the plight of the magnesium-exporting nations.

the behavior of others. Another breathlessly reveals
that a sense of humor and intelligence are not always
linked in humans. We are shown charts which prove
that jokes popular in Pakistan are not quite as funny
when retold on the streets of Toronto and are presented
with data which shows us that fat women in jokes get
more laughs than fat men, but that jokes about male
absentminded professors go over better than jokes
about their female counterparts. Others attend conferences to argue the extent to which jokes represent
aggression and hostility and to what degree they are
healthy. Still others debate the question of whether
laughter represents pleasure or displeasure — yet nobody seems willing to grapple with Robert Benchley's
position, taken in response to the humor scholarship
of his time, that laughter represents suppressed sneez-
ing.

— Finally, there is a growing utilitarian movement
in humor which has been sparked by such diverse
items as an Air Force study which determined that humor was good for military teamwork to Norm Cousins's
well-reported cure through laughter. Humor is in-
creasingly being seen as a powerful tool for enhancing
self-esteem, feedback, leadership, teamwork, caring,
sharing, tension-management, communicating, and all
the other late-twentieth-century talk-show verities.
These "discoveries" are often revealed by people who
act as if all of this were unknown to Will Rogers, James
Thurber, George Ade, and several million others op-
erating in the dark ages before electronic biofeedback
equipment.

There is, of course, nothing wrong with this save for
the fact that the solemnity of it all gets us away from
the humor — the jokes, laughs, and rubber noses.
"Humor," E. B. White once wrote, "can be dissected,
as a frog can, but the thing dies in the process and the
innards are discouraging to any but the pure scientific
mind." Touché. What follows amounts to a great army

of live frogs which have been trained to attack if you even think about dissection. With any luck you may experience what an early humor researcher described as

" . . . clonic spasms of the diaphragm in numbers ordinarily about 18 . . . while the skin at the outer canthi of the eyes is characteristically puckered . . . a marked proper flexion of the trunk for its relief . . . the eyes often slightly bulge forwards and the lachrymal gland becomes active."

Flies in the Soup

An old and important formula which dates back at least to the early days of vaudeville; it has inspired the following accolade from British humorist Michael Watts which appeared in his wonderfully corny book *I say, I say!*

"The diner who bawls 'Waiter, there's a fly in my soup!' is meat and drink to the Corny Jokester. He is the gagman's copy-book feed. 'Waiter, there's a fly in my soup!' surpasses, in my opinion, 'Why did the chicken cross the road?', 'Who was that lady I saw you with last night?' and all the rest, as the most prolific straight line in the history of Corn."

Watts paid further homage to the formula by listing sixteen replies. Not bad, but here are forty-three pure examples and sixty-nine variations, including a few stolen from Watts.

"Hey, waiter, there's a fly in my soup!"
   "Shhhhhh! Everyone will want one."

"Waiter, there's a fly in my soup!"
   "Don't apologize to me."

"Waiter, there's a fly in my soup!"
   "Half a fly would be worse."

"Waiter, there's a fly in my soup!"
   "At our restaurant, we guarantee you won't find a single fly."

"Whaddya mean?"
"Because they're all married."

"Waiter, there's a fly in my soup!"
  "That's all right, sir. No extra charge."

"Waiter, there's a fly in my soup!"
  "It can't be, sir, you're eating noon lunch . . . and
  this is a fly-by-night place."

"Waiter, there's a fly in my soup!"
  "That's all right. It's not hot enough to burn him."

"Waiter, there's a fly in my soup!"
  "Wring him out before you throw him away."

"Waiter, there's a fly in my soup!"
  "Yes, sir — better sip it with care."

"Waiter, there's a fly in my soup!"
  "So what! There's soup on your fly."

  Or:
  "Sir, you're fortunate there is no soup on your
  fly."

"Waiter, there's a fly in my soup!"
  "Okay, I'll bring you a fork."

"Waiter, there's a fly in my soup!"
  "I'm not the waiter, I'm the manager."

"Waiter, there's a fly in my soup!"
  "Force of habit, sir, the chef used to be a tailor."

"Waiter, there's a fly in my soup!"
  "Serves the chef right. I told him not to strain the
  broth through the fly swatter."

"Waiter, there's a fly in my soup!"
  "That's funny, there were two of them when I left
  the kitchen."

"Waiter, there's a fly in my soup!"
  "There's a fly that knows good soup."

"Waiter, there's a fly in my soup!"
"No, sir, that is an essential bee vitamin."

"Waiter, there's a fly in my soup!"
"Go ahead and eat him, there's more where he came from."

"Waiter, there's a fly in my soup!"
"Oh, hell! I've mixed my orders again."

"Waiter, there's a fly in my soup!"
"Don't worry, sir — he's a good swimmer."

"Waiter, there's a fly in my soup!"
"Funny — it's supposed to be mock-turtle."

"Waiter, there's a fly in my soup!"
"Don't worry, sir — he's only showing off."

"Waiter, there's a fly in my soup!"
"Nonsense, sir — we don't serve meat on Fridays."

"Waiter, there's a fly in my soup!"
"That's not a fly, sir, it's just dirt in the shape of a fly."

"Waiter, there's a fly in my soup!"
"Just a moment, sir — I'll fetch a spider."

"Waiter, there's a fly in my soup!"
"I know, watch him dive for the parsley."

"Waiter, there's a fly in my soup!"
"Well, do you blame him?"

"Waiter, there's a fly in my soup!"
"Okay, here's a fly swatter."

"Waiter, there's a fly in my soup!"
"That's not a fly, that's raisin delight."

"Waiter, there's a fly in my soup!"

"What do you expect with the blue plate? A hummingbird?"

"Waiter, there's a fly in my soup!"
"What did you expect for seventy-five cents, a Cornish game hen?"

"Waiter, there's a fly in my soup!"
"Does that mean that you'll be wanting dinner for two?"

"Waiter, there's a fly in my soup!"
"Sorry, I guess we forgot to put it on the menu."

"Waiter, there's a fly in my soup!"
"Don't worry, the frog should snap it up any second now."

"Waiter, there's a fly in my soup!"
"I know. It gives you a nice buzz doesn't it?"

"Waiter, there's a fly in my soup!"
"I'd like a second opinion."
"It's also too salty."

"Waiter, there's a fly in my soup!"
"Big deal! So you can identify aircraft."

"Waiter, there's a fly in my soup!"
"Just wait until you see the main course."

"Waiter, there's a fly in my soup!"
"That's strange. What kind of soup is it?"

"Waiter, there's a fly in my soup!"
"Ah, we've cornered him at last."

"Waiter, there's a fly in my soup!"
"Oh, don't mind him, he's just washing his tennis sneakers."

"Waiter, there's a fly in my soup!"

"If you wanted him with dessert, why didn't you say so?"

"Knock, Knock."
  "Who's there?"
  "Jupiter."
  "Jupiter who?"
  "Jupiter fly in my soup?"

"Waiter, there's a dead fly swimming in my soup!"
  "Nonsense, sir — dead flies can't swim."

"Waiter, what's this fly doing in my soup?"
  "Dunno, sir — looks like the breaststroke."

"Waiter, there's a fly swimming in my soup!"
  "You're lucky, sir — there's usually only enough for them to wade in."

"Waiter, there's a fly in the bottom of my soup bowl! What does this mean?"
  "Listen, Bud, if you want your fortune told, go see a gypsy."

Frog: "Waiter, there's no fly in my soup!"

"Waiter, what's that fly doing in this creamed soup?"
  "Trying to improve her complexion."

"Waiter, there's a spider in my soup!"
  "I'm sorry, sir, we must be out of flies."

"Waiter, there's a dead fly in my soup!"
  "I'm sorry, sir, I'm sure he was alive when he left the kitchen."

"Hey, waiter, what's this dead fly doing in my soup?"
  "It's the boiling water that kills them, sir."

"Waiter, there's a fly in my applesauce!"
"Of course, sir, it's a fruit fly."

"Waiter, there's a medfly in my soup!"
"I'm sorry sir, it should have been in your salad."

"Waiter, what is this fly doing in my alphabet soup?"
"Learning to read?"

"Waiter, there's a fly in my moo shu pork!"
"That's nothing. Wait until you open your fortune cookie."

"Waiter, there are pennies in my soup!"
"Well, sir, you said you'd stop eating here if there wasn't some change in the food."

"Waiter, there's a fly in my ice cream!"
"Serves him right, let him freeze to death."

"Waitress, there's a fly in my soup!"
"I think you want the waiter. I'm here for another joke."

"Waitress, do you have frog's legs?"
"No, I just broke the heel off my shoe."

"Waiter, there's a hair in my soup!"
"Is it blond, sir? We're missing a waitress."

"Waiter, do you have frog's legs?"
"Certainly, sir."
"Good. Hop into the kitchen and bring me a hamburger."

"Waiter, I must say that I don't like all the flies in this dining room!"

"Tell me which ones you don't like and I'll chase them out for you."

"Waiter, what's that in my soup?"
"I'd better call the manager, sir, I can't tell one insect from another."

"Waiter, there's a hair in my apple pie!"
"I can't understand it, sir. Those apples were Baldwins."

"Waiter, I don't like the looks of this trout!"
"If it's looks you're after, why didn't you order goldfish?"

"Hey, waiter, you've got your thumb in my bowl of soup!"
"Don't worry, sir, the soup isn't hot."

"Waiter!"
"Yes, sir, what can I do for you?"
"Waiter, I can't eat this stuff, call the manager!"
"It's no use. He won't eat it, either."

"Waiter, you advertise blended coffee here, but this stuff is terrible!"
"It is blended. It's a blend of yesterday's and today's."

"Waiter, you scratched the side of your nose with my spoon!"
"I'm sorry. Should I have used a fork instead?"

"Waiter, there's a caboose in my soup!"
"Yes, sir, this is a training table."

"Waiter, couldn't you make this corned beef lean?"
"Which way?"

"Waiter, take this steak back to the kitchen and tell the chef to chew it and choke!"

"I'm sorry sir, I can't. There are four cutlets, two chops, and a hamburger in front of you."

"Waiter, will those waffles be long?"
   "No, round."

"Waiter, this food isn't fit for a pig!"
   "All right, I'll get you some that is."

"Waiter, there's an ax in my soup!"
   "Naturally, sir, it's split pea."

"Waiter, I'd like a bowl of chili and a few kind words."
   "Here's the chili."
   "How about the kind words?"
   "Don't eat the chili."

"Waiter, how much longer do I have to keep on waiting!"
   "I'm waiting, you're just sitting there."

"Waiter, this chicken is as tough as a paving stone."
   "That's because it's a 'Plymouth Rock,' sir."

"Waiter, what's the difference between the blue-plate and the white-plate specials?"
   "The white plate is fifty cents more."
   "So the food is better?"
   "No, but we have to wash the plate."

"Waiter, how are your tongue sandwiches?"
   "They speak for themselves."

"Waiter, what happened to this lobster's other claw?"
   "He lost it in a fight."
   "Well, bring me the winner."

"Waiter, how do you serve shrimps here?"
   "We bend down."

"Waiter, I'll have the spaghetti. Will it be long?"
  "I don't know, we never measure it."

"Waiter, this plate is wet!"
  "That's your soup, sir."

"Waiter, this sausage has meat at one end and bread at the other."
  "Well, sir, you know how hard it is to make both ends meet these days."

"Waiter, this soup tastes like turpentine!"
  "It must be tea if it tastes like turpentine, because the soup tastes like kerosene."

"Waiter, I don't like this cheese!"
  "But it's Gruyère, sir."
  "Well, bring me some that grew elsewhere."

"Waiter."
  "Yes, sir."
  "What's this?"
  "It's your soup, sir."
  "Yes, but what kind?"
  "It's bean soup, sir."
  "I'm not asking what it has been, I'm asking what it is now."

"Waiter, this soup is spoiled!"
  "Who told you?"
  "A little swallow."

"Waiter, are there any eggs on your menu?"
  "No, I wiped them off."

"Waiter, I'm so hungry I could eat a horse!"
  "You certainly came to the right place."

"Waiter, I found a fly in the raisin bread!"
  "Okay, okay, I'll trade you for a raisin."

"Waiter, bring me some tomatoes."

"Stewed, sir?"
"None of your damn business."

"Waiter, does the chef have pig's feet?"
"I can't tell, he's got his shoes on."

"Waiter, what's this terrible tough stuff?"
"Sir, that's filet of sole."
"Go back and get me a nice tender piece from the top half of the shoe."

"Waiter, there's no chicken in my chicken soup."
"There's no horse in the horseradish, either."

"Waiter, this food gives me heartburn!"
"What did you expect in a restaurant, sunburn?"

"Waiter, there's a button in my soup!"
"Typographical error, sir, it should be mutton."

"Waiter, isn't this toast burnt?"
"No, sir, it just fell on the floor."

"Waiter, bring me some tomato juice for a pickup."
"Yes, sir, and what will you have for yourself?"

"Waiter, there's a hair in my soup!"
"Quite natural, sir, it's rabbit soup."

"Waiter, these eggs should be turned over."
"Turned over?"
"Turned over to the Museum of Natural History."

"Waiter, what's this fly doing in my soup?"
"About ten miles an hour."

"Waiter, do you serve crabs here?"
"We serve anyone; sit down."

"Waiter, there's a fly bothering me!"
"Shall I call a policeman, sir?"

"Waiter, there's a dead fly in my soup!"
"What do you want us to do, sir, have a funeral?"

"Waiter, just look at this chicken, it's nothing but
skin and bones!"
"All right, sir, I'll go get the feathers."

"Waiter, look at the chicken you just served me. One
leg is shorter than the other."
"Are you planning to eat it, sir, or dance with it?"

"Waiter, do you have eczema?" said the patron, no-
ticing the waiter scratching his face.
"No, sir, just what's on the menu."

Waiter: "Can I help you with your soup, sir?"
Diner: "Help me? What do you mean?"
Waiter: "Well, sir, from the sound I thought you
might wish me to drag you ashore."

"Flier, there's a weight in my soup."

At the Pearly Gates

As formulas go, it is one of our oldest. Early examples tend to remind us of grimmer times:

St. Peter: "Young man, how did you get here so quickly?"
Young man: "Flu."

In fact, it is hard to find a jokebook from any period, no matter how specialized, that does not have at least one pearly-gates joke. For instance, here is one from a 1915 automotive jokebook titled *Funabout Fords:*

St. Peter stood at the pearly gates and examined those who would enter. One of the questions he seemed to think important related to automobiles.

"What kind of car did you own?" he asked a large, portly soul.

"A Packard," replied the l.p.s.

"I am sorry," said St. Peter, "but that does not help you. You will have to go down."

"Did you have an auto?" he asked a long, lean bean.

"I did, sir — a Pierce-Arrow."

"Too bad," said St. Peter; "please press the lower button."

"And you, little man, did you own a machine?"

"Yes, sir, I did," replied a spry little fellow, starting to enter the elevator.

"What was it?"

"A Ford," replied the s.l.f.

"Come in," said St. Peter, throwing open the gates.
"You've had your hell on earth."

Starting with the next joke, which appears to be the
granddaddy of all pearly-gates stories, here is a roughly
chronological collection of them leading up to some
very recent examples.

A noted divine approaches the pearly gates and is
told that there is no room in heaven and that he will
have to wait for some years while new accommodations
are built.

He puts up a fuss and St. Peter finally tells him that
he will let him in on one provision: that he help solve
a major mystery. It seems that with millions crowded
into heaven they had lost track of Adam and Eve, who
were among their leading celebrities.

The minister says, "I'll be back in a few minutes."

St. Peter is stunned when he arrives a few minutes
later with a man and woman in tow.

"How were you able to find them?" says St. Peter.

"Simple! I just looked for a couple without navels."

"You're not due for another ten years," says St. Peter
to the new arrival. "Who's your doctor?"

> Most salesmen get in Heaven,
> In spite of how they rate —
> Before St. Peter spots them,
> A foot's inside the gate.

Woman: "I have come to join my husband."

St. Peter: "What was his name?"

Woman: "William Smith."

"That's hardly enough for me to identify him, as we
have many William Smiths here. Can you tell me anything else about him?"

"Well, just before he died he said that if I ever slept with another man, he'd turn over in his grave."

"Oh, you mean Whirling Willie."

The dead waiter's wife after many, many attempts contacts him through a medium.

"Sam, Sam, I can't believe it's really you," she says joyfully. "Speak to me."

A faint voice is heard: "I can't — it's not my table."

A stockbroker seeks admission to the pearly gates.

"Who are you?" says St. Peter.

"I am a Wall Street broker."

"What do you want?"

"I want to get in."

"What is it that entitles you to admission?"

"Well, for one thing, the other day I saw a decrepit old crone on Broadway and handed her a nickel."

"Is that in the records, Gabriel?"

"Yes, St. Peter."

"What else have you done?"

"Well, the other night I was crossing the Brooklyn Bridge and I ran into a half-frozen newsboy and I gave him a nickel."

"Gabriel, is that on the records?"

"Yes, St. Peter."

"What else have you done?"

"That's all I can think of."

"What do you think we ought to do with this guy, Gabriel?"

"Give him back his dime and tell him to go to hell."

An ardent golfer dies and finds himself at the pearly gates. St. Peter tells the man he has lived an exemplary life and that he can go right in.

The man asks, "St. Peter, where is the golf course?"

"I'm terribly sorry," replies St. Peter, "but that's one thing we don't have here."

The man turns and allows that he will see if the situation is any better in hell.

On the road to hell he is greeted by an imp who has already heard of the golfer's rejection of heaven.

"This way, sir," says the imp, "the finest tournament-quality eighteen holes you are likely to find this side of Augusta, Georgia."

The golfer looks around and agrees that it is the finest course he has ever seen.

"Fine," he says to the imp. "Get me some sticks and balls and I'll have the game of my life."

"I'm sorry, sir, we don't have any."

"What?" says the man. "No balls or clubs for a fine course like this?"

"No, sir," says the imp fiendishly, "that's the hell of it."

A bishop and a congressman arrive at the pearly gates. St. Peter greets them and says that he is going to give them immediate room assignments.

"Bishop, here are the keys to one of our nicest efficiency units. And for you Mr. Congressman, the keys to our finest penthouse suite."

"What?" says the bishop. "This is unfair."

"Listen," says St. Peter, "bishops are a dime a dozen up here, but this is the first congressman we've ever seen."

A woman goes to a medium in hopes that she will be able to communicate with the spirit of her late husband, Sam. The medium goes into a deep trance and after a while a voice says, "Emily, is that you?"

"Sam, I'd know your voice anywhere. How are you?"

"Fine."

"And how is it there — where you are?"

"Wonderful. Today the sky is deep blue, the temperature is perfect, and the grass is deep and high. And the cows are everywhere — beautiful cows of every color."

"Isn't that amazing," says Emily. "I had no idea there'd be cows in heaven."

"Heaven?" says Sam. "Who's talking about heaven? I'm a bull in Minnesota."

An oil company executive arrives at the pearly gates only to hear that the quota for oilmen has been met. St. Peter tells him, "The only possible way for you to enter is to somehow get one of the oilmen already here to leave."

The new arrival thinks for a while and then hits on the answer: he will create the rumor that oil has been discovered in hell and see if it will cause one of the oilmen in heaven to go over to the other side. St. Peter thinks it will be a good test and the rumor is planted.

Within a few hours there is a stampede through the pearly gates and all of the oilmen in heaven have bolted.

Suddenly an astonished St. Peter notices that the man who wanted to enter is starting to run in the direction of hell.

"Where are you going?" he calls.

Over his shoulder the man calls back, "Well there may be something to the report after all."

Three nuns perish in a bus wreck and shortly thereafter they all arrive at the pearly gates, where St. Peter greets them and says, "I'll ask each of you a question, and if you answer correctly I'll let you into heaven."

The first nun steps up and St. Peter asks, "Who was the first man on earth?"

"That's easy," she says. "Adam."

The gates open and she is admitted.

The second nun is asked the name of the first woman; she answers Eve and is admitted.

The third nun steps up and St. Peter says, "What did the first woman say to the first man when she first saw him?"

The nun starts, looks around despairingly, rolls her eyes, wrings her hands, and says, "Gee, that's a hard one!"

The clouds part and the gates open.

A man comes home to his apartment one day to find evidence that his wife has just been engaged in an extramarital romp. In fact the smell of the other man's cigar is still in the air.

Suddenly he gets the idea of trying to catch the guy. He runs out on the apartment's balcony, sees the cigar-smoking man leaving, runs back into the apartment, grabs the refrigerator, runs to the balcony, and drops it on the man with the cigar. The man who dropped the refrigerator then has a heart attack and dies.

Moments later three men approach the pearly gates. St. Peter begins by asking how each died.

"I was minding my own business when I was hit by a refrigerator," says the first man.

"I died from the exertion of lifting and carrying a refrigerator," says the second.

The third man steps forward and says, "I was hiding inside this refrigerator and . . . "

A nun, Sister Margaret, goes to heaven and finds that she must wait to gain admission.

St. Peter comes over and says to her, "Why don't you go back to earth and relax for a few weeks? Check in with me every week or so."

After a week she calls and says, "St. Peter, this is Sister Margaret. Everything is going well except for the fact that I smoked a cigarette."

"I think we can overlook that. Call me back next week."

The following week she calls and says, "Peter, this

is Margaret. . . . I had a few drinks last night, hope you don't mind."

St. Peter replies, "I think we can forgive you a few drinks. Your accommodations should be ready in a week or so."

A week later she calls again: "Pete, this is Meg. Forget it."

A pope dies and goes to heaven and is greeted by St. Peter. St. Peter explains that all is equal in heaven — no preference is ever given to anybody because of his earthly station. The pope says, "That's as it should be in heaven."

Later the pope is standing in the cafeteria line and a man wearing a white jacket with a stethoscope sticking out of the pocket walks to the front of the line and takes a tray.

"Did you see that?" the pope says to St. Peter. "You told me everyone was equal here."

"Oh, don't mind him," replies St. Peter. "That's God — he likes to play doctor once in a while."

A senator dies and goes to heaven. Upon passing through the pearly gates, he notices one of his Senate colleagues in the company of a most beautiful woman.

"Senator," says the newcomer, "it is indeed a pleasure to see a member of the world's greatest deliberative body rewarded so justly."

"Reward, hell," says the old senator. "I'm her punishment."

St. Peter has had a rough day and it occurs to Jesus Christ that he could use a little time off.

"Go get a cup of coffee," he says. "I can handle the pearly gates while you're gone."

St. Peter takes him up on the offer and Christ takes over. Nothing happens for the first few minutes, but then an old man comes shuffling up the path to heaven.

"What have you done to enter the kingdom of heaven?" He asks rather routinely.

"Not much," says the old man. "I am just a poor carpenter who has led a quiet life. The only remarkable thing about my life was my son."

"Your son?" Christ asks with obvious interest.

"Yes, he was quite a son. He went through a most unusual birth and later a great transformation. He also became known throughout the world and is still loved by many."

Christ looks at the man, embraces him tightly, and says, "Father, father!"

The old man hugs him back and asks, "Pinocchio?"

Three Jews arrive at the pearly gates and St. Peter greets them by saying, "Fellows, we're running short on space so I'm going to ask you some questions, and just to make it tough they will be about other religions. If you answer correctly, you get right in, but if you make a mistake, you will have to wait."

The first man is asked to tell the story of the life of Buddha.

"I won't even try," he says as he heads off toward the waiting area.

The same thing happens when the second man is asked to describe the life of Mohammed.

But when the third man is asked to tell the life of Jesus Christ he tells the story in absolutely perfect detail from the moment of his birth to his crucifixion.

"That's absolutely remarkable," says St. Peter, adding, "There are very few priests who could tell it as well as you just did. But you're not done. Please, sir, what happened after the crucifixion?"

"Well, sir, he is buried in a cave, but on the morning of the third day the stone rolls away from the mouth of the cave. At this moment he rises out of the tomb and if he sees his shadow, that means we will have six more weeks of winter."

Two priests are killed in an automobile accident. Upon arriving at the pearly gates they are informed that the computer is down and that they will have to go back to earth for a week.

"Fellows," says St. Peter, "you can go back as anything you'd like and because the computer is down, nothing will count against you."

The first priest tells St. Peter that he had always dreamt of being an eagle, soaring over the Rocky Mountains.

"Go," says St. Peter. "You're an eagle."

The second priest first reconfirms the fact that whatever he does will not go into his record and then says, "Well, I've always wanted to be a stud."

"Go," says St. Peter. "You're a stud."

A week passes and the archangel Gabriel comes to St. Peter to say that the computer is now back in operation and it is now time for him to go and fetch the two priests.

"Well," says St. Peter, "the first guy will be easy to find. He's flying over the Rockies near the Colorado-Wyoming border. The other guy's going to be a lot harder to find: he's somewhere inside a snow tire in Minnesota."

The gate between heaven and hell breaks and St. Peter calls over to the devil, "It's your turn to fix it."

"Sorry," says the devil. "We are too busy fixing our heating system to worry about a little thing like a gate."

"If you don't fix it," says St. Peter, "I'll have to sue you for breaking our working agreement."

"Is that so?" says the devil. "Where are you going to find a lawyer?"

St. Peter greets a lawyer at the Pearly Gates with unusual warmth.

"Gee," says the lawyer. "Does everybody get this kind of treatment?"

"You're not just anyone," Saint Peter replies. "We seldom get lawyers who are as distinguished and old as you."

"But I'm only 48," says the lawyer.

"Funny," says St. Peter. "You've billed for so many hours we thought you were 80."

The Lowest Form of the Lowest Form

If the pun is the lowest form of humor — also the lowest form of pastry — the lowest form of pun is the knock-knock joke. This is what makes them so appealing. They have some remarkable qualities. For one, they defy scholarly analysis and those who try to find meaning in them are destined to bog down in mindless babble within a sentence or two. ("They are joking parables of comic tentativeness and psychological expansion," wrote one analyst, who obviously never said, "Disraeli who? Disraeli too much.")

The paradox ("Paradox who? Paradox better than one if you're really sick") is that while they defy intellectualizing they are intellectually demanding. This very point was made by John F. Gilbey (the pseudonym of a closet Knocker who has sworn me to secrecy), who wrote, "Some will snort at this, but what do they know? They are the same species who believe that chess is more cerebral than checkers. For them, solve this: Pirhana . . . What'd I tell you. It's tough. But to veteran knockers used to cosmic cerebration it's no problem: 'Pirhana old gray bonnet . . .'" Gilbey also believes that the reason why knock-knocks have resisted the full press of a major fad is that they are intellectually too demanding for most.

They are also extremely satisfying both in the reciting and, for those with the gift, in the creating. To create a really first-rate knock-knock is the mental equivalent of a golfer's hole-in-one. Sit back and listen to the testimonials:

J.C.Y., Sr., a lawyer from Williamsport, Pennsylvania, recalls,

> In 1934 when I was thirty-one years old I was a delegate to the annual meeting of the American Bar Association in Milwaukee, Wisconsin. Knock-knock jokes were at their height. I had occasion to use the men's room at my hotel. Upon returning to the lobby I ran into a lawyer friend from Phil-adelphia. I don't know why but something I had just seen inspired me. I said, "Knock, knock." My friend replied, "Who's there?" I said, "Ranger," and he said, "Ranger who?" I said, "Ranger clothes before leaving the men's room."

It is hard to think of better testimonial to any form of humor than an eighty-year-old man's ability to recall a joke he'd made up forty-nine years earlier; but there are others which come close.

Mike Thaler, who has written a number of knock-knock jokes and is the reigning "Riddle King," says this:

> Kids just go crazy over them. You stand in front of a room full of them and say "Knock-knock" and you are almost knocked over by the roar of "Who's there?" You know the one that they love the most?
> Knock, Knock.
> Who's there?
> Honda.
> Honda who?
> Your hondaware is showing.

Before moving on, it is only right that we introduce the knock-knock which Thaler feels is his personal best:

Knock, Knock.
Who's there?
Energize.
Energize who?
Her hair is blond energize are blue.

If you look hard enough, other important bits of testimonial show up . . . and at the most opportune moments. On a Friday afternoon in September 1981 I was
stuck in the airport in Hartford, Connecticut, waiting
for a long-delayed plane. I began amusing myself by
studying the local phone books, racking my brain looking for new knock-knock ideas. Suddenly it hit me.
Here I was a man in my forties, in a suit, standing next
to a phone booth trying to figure out whether the name
Rocco Spanducci could be turned into a serviceable
knock-knock joke.

The absurdity of it all troubled me and I walked away
thinking of friends who were, at that very moment,
healing the sick or defending the innocent. At that moment it was clear that a Nobel was forever outside my
reach. Sitting dejectedly, I tried to think of something
else and picked up a few loose pages from a copy of
the previous day's *Hartford Courant*. I started reading
an article on Roald Dahl by a local free-lancer named
Susan Slavet and there were the lines from Dahl which
I have now committed to memory: "I'm sixty-five and
really just an adolescent. When I meet other fellows
my age I think, 'There but for the grace of God go I.'
I adore 'Knock-knock' jokes."*

To hell with the Nobel (Nobel's no blue chips), I
reasoned, thinking of the prolonged adolescence of
Roald Dahl.

---

*According to the article of September 17, 1981, Dahl's favorite:
    Knock, Knock.
    Who's there?
    Humphrey.
    Humphrey who?
    Humphrey ever blowing bubbles.
Dahl added, "I love that one. No one can ever figure it out."

Roald Dahl
Roald Dahl who?
Roald Dahl the barrel. We'll have a barrel of fun.

The most important force in contemporary knockery is William Cole, the poet and anthologist, who has published several knock-knock books and has six more on their way. He reports — you heard it here first — ". . . the beginnings of a NAUGHTY KNOCK KNOCK BOOK ("U Thant lay me if you don't pay me!" "Vonnegut into your pants tonight!") Like that."*

Cole has not only functioned as an important collector and promoter of the form, but has created some of the genre's modern classics. His favorite original:

Knock, Knock.
Who's there?
Amaryllis.
Amaryllis who?
Amaryllis state agent—wanna buy a house?

Not only did he pen the original but he even came up with his own variation:

Knock, Knock.
Who's there?
Amarillo.
Amarillo who?
Amarillo-fashioned cowboy.

---

*Cole's book of naughty knock-knocks will doubtlessly open up a whole new front. One of rare few examples I have heard comes from my good friend, writer Joseph C. Goulden:
Knock, Knock.
Who's there?
Fornication.
Fornication who?
Fornication like this, you should wear black tie.

It can be argued, however, that Cole's single greatest contribution has been his uncovering of a major historical item. Dorothy Parker may well have invented the knock-knock joke. Cole came on this while reading Edmund Wilson's *The Twenties*, and he then got off a report which was published in *The New York Times* on October 20, 1982. With Cole's permission, here are the words which knocked the knock-knock world on its ear:

There's a passage — and this was in 1920, mind you — where Wilson is discussing (and generally dismissing) the Algonquin Round Table. He writes: "At one time their favorite game consisted of near-punning use of words. 'Have you heard Dotty's "Hiawatha" — "Hiawatha nice girl till I met you." ' Marc Connelly's 'Honduras': something about 'the big Honduras [endurance] contest.' Somebody else's Benchley: 'Benchley [eventually]? Why not now?' (This was an advertising slogan.)" A later entry in Wilson's diary discusses Miss Parker, giving a couple of really bad knock-knocks, and this rather good one:

Knock, Knock.
Who's there?
Scrantoknow.
Scrantoknow who?
Scrantoknow you're appreciated.
"Dorothy," Mr. Wilson says, "thought they were not right unless the word began the sentence. . . ."

Cole admits that they weren't actually called knock-knocks and argues that the key word must appear at the beginning of the punch line; but these are minor points. Before this, it had always been assumed that the jokes were created by college students in the 1930s. It would now appear that the 1930s was the period in which they came into their own. During the early Depression years the movement grew slowly.

Then, in the summer of 1936, it became what *The Literary Digest* termed America's "newest nonsense craze" with knock-knocks ringing "in everyone's ears." It hit first in the colleges in May and was carried forward by orchestra leader Vincent Lopez, who composed and recorded a song "Knock Knock Who's There," containing some of the most popular examples, and got no fewer than five thousand letters with knock-knocks he had left out. Hal Kemp also made a record of the Lopez song, Paramount made a short knock-knock comedy, and the Dell Publishing Company published the first knock-knock book.* Newspapers offered cash prizes for the best knock-knocks and any columnist worthy of the name found a way to work a few into his column. Heywood Broun made up this one:

> Knock, Knock.
> Who's there?
> A gang of vigilantes with machine guns, leather and brass knuckles to thump anybody who persists in playing this fool knock-knock game.

Before it was all over, CBS had banned the song from its live radio shows after a few suggestive puns had been worked into versions of the song and Whitney Bolton, a columnist for the New York *Morning Telegraph*, had termed it "a mental disease."

For knock-knocks there was never to be another 1936, but the form never went into eclipse, either. They became as much a ritual of childhood as marbles and hopscotch had been to earlier generations and there were always adults who, as John Gilbey put it, couldn't

---

*That book, *Knock, Knock*, by Bob Dunn, which originally cost a dime, has become one of the hardest-to-find items of knock-knock memorabilia. The Library of Congress doesn't even have a copy, nor does the San Francisco Public Library, which houses the nation's largest public collection of humor books.

hear the word *Avon* without thinking of Garbo (Avon to be alone) or hear *aardvark* without thinking of Al Jolson (Aardvark a million miles for one of her smiles . . .).

Today there are an astonishing number and variety of knock-knocks. One man, whom we will meet a bit later, has collected 131,000 of them and they come in a number of variant forms, including:

The Novelty Knock-Knock
    Knock, Knock.
    Who's there?
    It is I.
    Oh, a Harvard man.

The Triple Comeback
    Knock, Knock.
    Who's there?
    Eskimo, Christian, Italian.
    Eskimo, Christian, Italian who?
    Eskimo, Christian, Italian no lies.

The Shaggy Knock-Knock
    Will you remember me in five years?
    Yes.
    Will you remember me next year?
    Yes.
    Will you remember me next month?
    Yes.
    Will you remember me next week?
    Yes.
    Will you remember me tomorrow?
    Yes.
    Will you remember me in another minute?
    Yes.
    Will you remember me in another second?
    Yes.
    Knock, Knock.

Who's there?
You forgot me already?

The Special Occasion Knock
   Knock, Knock.
   Who's there?
   Sensuous.
   Sensuous who?
   Sensuous such a nice person, I wish you a happy
   birthday.

The Celebrity Knock
   Knock, Knock.
   Who's there?
   Baloney.
   Baloney who?
   Baloney God can make a tree.

This is a celebrity knock-knock which was solicited
from William Safire initially to test the premise that
the busier and brighter the person, the more likely he
is to have a fine knock-knock joke at the forefront of
his brain. Safire's response proves this beyond any
shadow of a doubt.

The Series Knock-Knock
   Knock, Knock.
   Who's there?
   Ether.
   Ether who?
   Ether bunny.

   Knock, Knock.
   Who's there?
   Stella.
   Stella who?
   Stella nother Ether bunny.

Knock, Knock.
Who's there?
Samoa.
Samoa who?
Samoa Ether bunnies.

Knock, Knock.
Who's there?
Consumption.
Consumption who?
Consumption be done about these Ether bunnies?

Scattered in the pages ahead are three collections of knock-knock jokes, each of which appears as a full-blown chapter. They have been seeded this way for the obvious reason: their aforementioned intellectual richness is such that it would be too much to have them all at once — the cerebral equivalent of three hot-fudge sundaes.

"Doc . . . Next"

Imagine one of the Marx Brothers as your doctor and the scene is set for one of the simplest and eternally accurate formulas. A quick, healthy dose for this age of high-speed medicine:

"Doc, you're charging me ten dollars and all you did was paint my throat."
"What did you expect for ten dollars — wallpaper? Next."

"Doc, what should I do if my temperature goes up another point?"
"Sell! Next."

"Doc, how can I avoid falling hair?"
"Step to one side. Next."

"Doc, should I file my nails?"
"No. Throw them away like everybody else. Next."

"Doc, I just wanted to let you know that there is an invisible man in your waiting room."
"Tell him I can't see him now. Next."

"Doc, you've gotta do something for me. I snore so loudly that I wake myself up."
"In that case, sleep in another room. Next."

"Doc, my hair is coming out. What can you give me to keep it in?"

"A cigar box. Next."

"Doc, my child just swallowed a pen. What should I
do?"
"Use a pencil. Next."

"Doc, is it a boy?"
"Well, the one in the middle is. Next."

"Doc, what am I really allergic to?"
"Paying my bills. Next."

"Doc, every bone in my body hurts."
"Be glad you're not a herring. Next."

"Doc, what would you take for this cold?"
"Make me an offer. Next."

"Doc, there's something wrong with my stomach."
"Keep your coat buttoned and nobody will notice
it. Next."

"Doc, there's a man outside with a wooden leg
named Smith."
"What's the name of his other leg? Next."

"Doc, am I getting better?"
"I don't know — let me feel your purse. Next."

"Doc, am I going to die?"
"That's the last thing you're going to do. Next."

"Doc, how long will I live?"
"You should live to be eighty."
"I am eighty."
"What did I tell you? Next."

"Doc, this ointment you gave me makes my arm
smart."
"Why not rub some on your head? Next."

"Doc, what should I do? I can't sleep at night."
"Sleep during the day. Next."

"Doc, what's the difference between an itch and an
allergy?"
"About twenty-five dollars. Next."

"Doc, don't you think I should get a second opinion?"
"Sure. Come back tomorrow. Next."

"Doc, nobody can figure out what's wrong with me.
I've got the oddest collection of symptoms."
"Have you had it before?"
"Yes."
"Well, you've got it again. Next."

"Doc, I think I've developed a split personality."
"Okay, go chase yourself. Next."

"Doc, I'm feeling a bit schizophrenic."
"That makes four of us. Next."

"Doc, can you give me something for my head?"
"No thanks, I've already got one. Next."

"Doc, I think I've got a bad liver."
"Well, take it back to the butcher. Next."

"Doc, what's your best suggestion for this terrible
halitosis of mine?"
"Lockjaw. Next."

"Doc, I get this terrible pain in my back every time
I bend over."
"Then don't bend over. Next."

"Doc, what should I take when I get run down?"
"The license number. Next."

"Doc, nobody ever listens to me."
"Next."

Punintended

Obscene verse.
> — Alleged comment about a lewd poem,
> Ben Jonson

A man who could make so vile a pun would not scruple to pick a pocket.
> — John Dennis

I never knew an enemy of puns who was not an ill-natured man. A pun is a noble thing per se; it fills the mind, it is as perfect as a sonnet. May my last breath be drawn through a pipe and exhaled in a pun.
> — Charles Lamb

Punning is a talent which no man affects to despise but he that is without it.
> — Jonathan Swift

. . . those most dislike puns who are least able to utter them.
> — Edgar Allan Poe

A good pun may be admitted among the smaller excellencies of lively conversation.
> — James Boswell

One of the surest signs of crass insensitivity and general boorishness is a dislike of puns. Proof is at hand.

During a portion of Beethoven's Ninth in which there are no bass violin parts, one of the bassists passes a bottle of Scotch around. The bass section become totally looped, but the conductor is unaware of what is going on. His assistant decides he must let him know and hands him this note:

"Top of the Ninth, basses loaded."

A notoriously surly and boorish baseball umpire returns home after a long road trip. He settles into his easy chair and calls his little boy over to sit on his lap. "No," says the lad, "the son never sits on the brutish umpire."

A man comes home to find a notorious Czechoslovakian philanderer coming out of his wife's bedroom. He chases him down the hall, out the window, and down the fire escape.

On his way down the philanderer jumps into another apartment and says to the surprised tenant, "Can you cache a small Czech?"

A Spanish mother and a Jewish father name their daughter Carmen Cohen. The mother only addresses her as Carmen and the father will only call her Cohen with the result that she never knew if she was Carmen or Cohen.

In order to forget his terrible hangover, a man goes hunting. Almost immediately a large rabbit jumps out of the brush and grabs hold of his dog's leg with his teeth. The man shoots the rabbit and rushes home to stew it. The hangover disappears with the first bite, which was the piece of the hare that bit the dog.

All the top chess players arrive at a hotel for an international tournament. They spend the first hour or so standing around the lobby telling each other of recent victories. Without warning, the hotel manager throws them all out of the lobby and tells them to go to their rooms.
When asked why, he says, "If there's one thing I can't stand it's chess nuts boasting by an open foyer."

An Indian rajah becomes so selfish about hunting that he forbids all his subjects from the sport.
Angered, they rise up and overthrow him, making this the first time a reign was called because of game.

Scientists have found a tribe of half a thousand women in India who were born without nipples. Perhaps you've heard of them by their more common name: the India Nippleless 500.

A light-bulb manufacturer announces that he will give away free bulbs to any theater owner who uses them on his marquee.
"This is madness," says his accountant.
"I know, but I've always wanted to see my lights up in names."

Two servicemen in Africa are bragging about which is the better lion hunter. They bet a pint of beer on the outcome of a contest to see which is the first to bag a lion. The first man sets off on foot while the second goes to a nearby air base, where he borrows a jet. The man in the jet sights a lion and shoots it.

As he claims his prize he points out that a strafed lion is the shortest distance between two pints.

A hospital patient who had refused to have his temperature taken was finally asked by the head nurse why he would not cooperate. His answer: "On the springs, the young man's fanny politely spurns the shove."

Year in and year out a doctor stops by a bar on the way home from work and orders a daiquiri with a walnut in it. One day the bartender sees the doctor approaching, reaches for a walnut, and finds that there are none. He rushes around the bar until he finds an old hickory nut which he tosses in the glass.

The doctor takes one sip, grimaces, and bellows, "What the hell is this?"

The bartender meekly replies, "A hickory-daiquiri, Doc."

The Milwaukee Brewers cannot win against Milt Famey, a pitcher who is normally mediocre but a terror against them. It is late in the season and the Brewers need a win badly, but they are facing Famey the next day. They hit on a plan. One of the team's front-office men will arrive at Famey's hotel, pose as a fan, and try to get Famey drunk on beer. The plan works to the extent that Famey drinks ten bottles of beer with the "fan."

The next day, however, Famey is perfect through eight innings and the Brewers' only solace is that the other team is also scoreless. Then in the ninth Famey walks four successive batters, which eventually gives the Brewers a 1–0 victory.

Later in the locker room there is a toast: "Here's to Schlitz, the beer that made Milt Famey walk us."

"I would like to reaffirm my belief in Buddha," said the Oriental gentleman, "but there is a great deal to be said for margarine."

A professor of Greek takes his torn suit to a Greek tailor. The tailor looks at the pants and says, "Euripides?"
"Yes," replies the professor, "Eumenides."

A noted dog trainer gives a party in honor of his most talented animal, a spaniel. As part of the festivities the spaniel sits down at a baby grand and begins playing a Bach sonata. During the recital one of the guests begins to talk loudly and the dog growls and chases the noisy guest out of the room.
"Don't worry," the trainer shouts nervously, "his Bach is worse than his bite."

A woman opened her refrigerator and spied a rabbit there.
Woman: What are you doing in my icebox?
Rabbit: This is a Westinghouse, isn't it?
Woman: Yes.
Rabbit: I'm just Westing.

"Terrible day," said the Great Dane as he complained to his master. "Work was bad, but then I got on the bus and it was completely packed with small dogs."
"Well," replied the master, "that's what you get for riding during peke hours."

"Dad, what is that over there underneath the funny-looking beast?"
"There's nothing, son, under the gnu."

Two racehorses, meeting at Santa Anita, eye each other for a moment.

"Don't I know you?" says one.

"I think so. I don't recall your name but the pace is familiar."

Two goats are busy eating garbage. One finds a roll of old film and chews it up.

"Did you enjoy the film?"

"Actually, I preferred the book."

"If your father could see you now," said the mother turkey to her errant son, "he'd turn over in his gravy."

Two frogs were sitting on a lily pad. One leaned over to the other and said, "Time sure is fun when you're having flies."

Two snakes are talking about the social airs being put on by an old acquaintance.

"Just think," says one, "I knew her back when she didn't have a pit to hiss in."

Two microbes become bored with life in the lymph system of a horse and move into the animal's blood system, where they are immediately killed by a dose of penicillin.

Moral: Don't change streams in the middle of a horse.

A dentist becomes completely obsessed by floss. His compulsion becomes so great that he buys a roan horse to help him gather floss for his growing collection. Another dentist becomes even more compulsive and steals the first man's horse, but the horse refuses to help him.

Moral: A stolen roan gathers no floss.

Three Indian women were all preparing to have babies. To make them comfortable, the chief asked each one what kind of animal skin she wanted to bear her baby on. The first chose a bearskin, the second requested an elk hide, and the third asked for the hide of a hippopotamus.

They all gave birth. The first had a five-pound son, the second a six-pound son, and the third had an eleven-pound baby boy.

All of this goes to prove that the son of the squaw on the hippopotamus is equal to the sons of the squaws on the other two hides.

There once was this little snail who loved fast sports cars. He bought himself a red Porsche and painted a big red S on each door. One day while going down the highway at a hundred miles per hour, he was spotted by a state trooper, who said to his partner, "Brother, look at that S-car go!"

A Datsun owner finds that he is in need of a special cog for his car's engine. It is a very early model car and he is told that he must have a cog specially built at the Datsun factory and must buy a minimum of one hundred of them. Since the car won't work without the part, he reasons that he has no choice but to buy all one hundred of them. So eager is he to get the cogs that he flies to Japan and brings them back with him in his lap. As the plane is crossing the U.S., the pilot announces engine trouble and orders the passengers to jettison all extra weight. The man slips one of the cogs into his pocket and throws the other ninety-nine overboard.

On the ground a farm couple is just sitting down to dinner. The wife looks out the window and says to her husband, "Look, Fred, its raining Datsun cogs."

A man is stricken with the oddest affliction: whenever he breaks wind, it makes the sound "honda." He finally asks his doctor about it. The doctor exhausts all the references in the literature and is just about to conclude that there is no answer when he is hit with a brainstorm. "I will call Honda in Japan and talk to the company doctor."

He talks with the Japanese doctor about the problem and he says, "Check to see if your patient has a dental infection — an abscess."

The patient is checked and sure enough there is an infection. It is treated and the affliction ends.

But the American doctor is haunted by the ability of his Japanese counterpart to diagnose the problem from such a distance and finally calls him on the phone.

"Doc, how did you know?"

"Simple," replies the Japanese doctor. "Abscess makes fart go 'honda.' "

In ancient Greece, Zeus visits a young man named Benny and tells him he can be immortal if he agrees to remain unshaven.

"If you shave," says the king of the gods, "you will burn and your ashes will remain forever in an urn."

All goes well for centuries, but one day in the twentieth century he falls in love with a woman who insists that he shave.

He figures that Zeus has forgotten by now and shaves. The ancient curse is immediately carried out.

Moral: A Benny shaved is a Benny urned.

Mercy Hospital in Chicago is run by a group of nuns, originally from Australia. Over the years they have gone out of their way to maintain ties with their native land— for instance, there is a gigantic map of Australia in the main reception area and they serve Australian tea from tins with koala bears on the outside.

One night a patient calls in the head nurse to let her know how much he loves the hospital.

"Sir, are you trying to tell me that there is nothing here that you don't like?" she says.

The man thinks for a moment and finally says, "Things are so good here that the only thing that I can think of to complain about is the fact that I got some leaves in my tea the other night."

"Ah," she replies. "The koala tea of Mercy is not strained."

A man becomes totally fed up with his mean and vicious horse and shoots him. He sells the flesh but finds nobody will buy the bones. He rows the bones out to the center of a lake and just as he is about to dump them a wind blows up, capsizes the boat, and the man drowns.

Moral: People who live with cross horses shouldn't row bones.

The monastery was having its annual smelt fry with beer, chips, and all the trimmings. A stranger stopped in the hopes of getting a bite to eat and asked the first man he saw, "Are you the fish friar?"

"No," the brother answered, "I'm the chip monk."

A famous actor was attending the public cremation of a close friend when he was accosted by a fan who kept asking him annoying questions. In order to get away from the pest, he began to run; but he stumbled and fell into the fire. Recovering from his burns in the hospital, he remarked, "Just one more case of going from the prying fan into the pyre."

After scientists perfected the cloning technique, they decided that each person should have a copy, which would be stored until the original person died, at which point the copy would carry on.

At first it was decided that the clones would be made in alphabetical order. However, many people without relatives argued that they should have priority so that they could carry on their names. The scientists decided this was fair and decreed, "Let him who is without kin stash the first clone."

An aging movie actor who has always done his own stunts decides it is time to get a stand-in and hits on the novel idea of getting a clone of himself.

Secretly, and at great cost, he has it done and the plan is a great success as the clone takes all the risks and bruises.

However, one day the actor is surprised when the clone bursts into his penthouse apartment swearing and yelling at him. The actor tries to calm the clone, but to no avail. Finally the clone becomes so agitated that he physically attacks the actor. The actor deftly stops the attack and manages to cause the other man to fall off the penthouse balcony to his death.

Ten minutes later a policeman arrives and tells the actor that he is under arrest.

"Arrest for what?" asks the actor. "That was not a real person, hence the charge of murder will not obtain. Try and charge me!"

The policeman thought for a moment and then said, "I've got it: I'm charging you with making an obscene clone fall."

Too Much Saxon Violence

At the time this project was started there were certain pun forms which were not immediately apparent to the author, but which had to be suggested by others with a better ear for what was classic. A few examples:

The missing/extra letter proverb. Jeffrey H. Goldstein, professor of psychology at Temple University and coeditor of *The Handbook of Humor Research* and *The Psychology of Humor,* finds it impossible to leave common phrases alone. Here are some which he has modified by a single letter:

> *Home is where you hang your cat.*
> *Home is where the heat is.*
> *Love is ever having to say you're sorry.*
> *A fool and his monkey are soon parted.*
> *You can't make a money out of me.*

The possibilities are endless, just as they are with:
Little-known Towns. Russell J. Dunn, Sr., of Lakewood, Ohio, plays with a number of formats including this one:

Shapeless, Mass.	Ooola, La.
Goodness, Me.	Income, Tex.
Deathly, Ill.	Hittor, Miss.
Praise, Ala.	Coco, Colo.
Proan, Conn.	Farmerina, Del.
Inert, Mass.	Noaz, Ark.
Nohitznorunzno, Ariz.	Lowe, Cal.

Deeba, Cal.
Nevah, Mo.
Goinga, Ga.
Ether, Ore.
Sayno, Mo.

Acapel, La.
Sweetasapls, Ida.
Doremifaso, La.
Sheza, Tenn.
Carr, Wash.
Hezmakinizatme, Pa.

Dunn also varies that format — Troy a little tenderness, Helena hand basket, Billings and cooings, Topeka out of the torn sock, Spokane like a gentleman, Orlando the free, Fairbanks pay interest, Cheyenne never has a date, and Juneau the way to San Jose?

There were other examples, but clearly the most habit-forming was a new form from the fertile mind and files of an Illinois woman named N. Sally Hass. One would be hard pressed to find a better example of the "degenerative pun" than these that take their cue from this simple question and answer:

Why did they ban The Story of O?
Too much sex and violence.
Degeneration then sets in.

Why did they ban *Ivanhoe?*
Too much Saxon violence.

Why did they ban the story of the compulsive eater who sold germ-contaminated secondhand microscopes to finance his addiction?
Too much snacks and vile lenses.

Why did they ban the story of the mother who worked her fingers to the bone knitting hosiery to pay for her son's music lessons?
Too much socks and violins.

Why did they ban the story of the thirteen drunken interior decorators who managed to hang the wrong color drapery fabric over every single window frame of a forty-two-room mansion?

Too much soaks and valances.

Why did they ban the story of the doctor who cured the soprano's laryngitis by having her massage her throat with VapoRub and refrain from singing a note or speaking a word for an entire month?

Too much Vicks and silence.

Why did they ban the story of the Middle Eastern ladies who protested against Western immodesty by dressing in their traditional chadors, marching into all the bazaars, and refusing to leave?

Too much sugs and veil-ins.

Why did they ban the story of the spoiled-rotten princess who stood at her window for three days and pouted at the mobs of upper-grade serfs who were attacking the castle?

Too much sulks and villeins.

Why did they ban the story of the loony bin—excuse me, the mental health facility—where half the patients insisted that they were really Charlie (The Bird) Parker and the other half went around all day muttering, "Where are the snows of yesteryear?"?

Too much sax and Villon.

Why did they ban the story of the mother fox who was so jealous and possessive of her cubs that, every time one of them went out on a date, she would surreptitiously sabotage his appearance by sneakily sticking bits of dandelion and milkweed fluff to his coat?

Too much vixen's sly lints.

Given such a display, it is hard to resist adding one of one's own. Here's mine:

Why did the National Football League attempt to discourage overly macho razor-blade ads which featured professional football players?
Too much Schicks and virulence.

All of this suggests many other possibilities for the dedicated, degenerative punster. "Nothing is certain but death and taxes," in the mouth of an owl, becomes ". . . death and taxidermists" for openers, and one can turn a line like "A sad but excusable slip of the tongue" into a major piece of foolishness. A friend suggests the song *"Guantanamera"* as a gold mine of sung punch lines ("One-ton tomato," "Wantin' to mate oh," "Wanton tomato," etc.) and for the world-class punster there is the challenge of the next chapter.

The Chattanooga Challenge

Jokes with kickers which rely on punned titles and lines from well-known songs are hardly uncommon, as shown by these fine examples:

A witch doctor tells one of his patients that the only cure he can suggest for the man's stomachache is to take a leather thong, cut it into twelve equal pieces, and swallow one each day.

Twelve days later he returns. "It's no use Doc. The thong is gone, but the malady lingers on."

Tina, the Hollywood agent, was so upset by her inability to find work for a singer that she began to sob for her in her presence.

Her client tried to console her. "Don't cry for me, Agent Tina."

As fine as these are, however, they pall in comparison to the jokes which rely on a line from the song which one reporter once said "very nearly became America's second national anthem during World War II."

It all started in 1974 when Glenn Collins of *The New York Times* got wind of a new joke form. He valiantly tried to find its source. He recalls today, "Never could track it down. Went through three people and tracked it to someone's teen-age son, who couldn't remember where he heard it." Remarkably, nobody has yet stepped forward to take credit for this discovery.

With the help of the *Times* advertising columnist
Philip H. Dougherty, who had tipped Collins to this
important joke phenomenon, a major collection was
assembled and published in *The New York Times
Magazine* of January 19, 1975.

Collins thought that it would become an overnight
sensation and today seems a bit disappointed that his
craze "seems to have left no residue."

His disappointment may be ill founded, however, as
this joke collector keeps coming up with evidence that
it has had a profound influence on some dedicated
punsters who dream of coming up with a story which
ends with a play on the line "Pardon me, boy, is this
the Chattanooga Choo-Choo?" One devotee, Dr.
Howard F. Heller of Omak, Washington, points out that
the challenge is not for everyone:

"With most formula jokes most people groan and try
to top the last joke (as opposed to just groaning) but
the Chattanooga Choo-Choo joke is rarely tackled by
those who hear it. One in a hundred might try."

There is other evidence that the struggle continues.
In May of 1983 an appeal for these jokes was broadcast
on radio station WIND in Chicago by Norman Mark.
There were a number of duplicates and slight variations
on known versions as well as several new ones.

Here are eight from Collins's original collection plus
four new versions.

1. According to a wholly unsubstantianted rumor repeated in White House circles shortly after former
President Nixon retired to his San Clemente estate, it
seems that only hours after his arrival in California,
Mr. Nixon telephoned Gerald Ford. When the new
President got on the line, Mr. Nixon is unreliably reported to have said:

"Pardon me, boy, this is the chap who knew to
choose you."

2. As he was leaving the zoo, a visitor walked by the gnu cage and noticed an unkempt gnu sitting morosely in a corner. Outside the cage was a large bamboo shoot with teeth marks on it. Thinking the gnu might have thrown it out of the cage, the visitor turned to an attendant and said:

"Pardon me, boy, is this the shoddy gnu's bamboo shoot?"

3. (This is unquestionably the most popular example.) Roy Rogers, cowboy star, finally took delivery of his long-awaited pair of custom boots — made with crocodile skin inlaid with silver and precious stones. Roy had never before had such a pair of boots, and he'd owned 1,276. Slipping them on, he decided to give them a trial ride on the range, and as he rode, he kept looking from right to left, admiring the beauty of his footwear.

Suddenly an angry cougar leaped from behind a huge boulder. With a single swipe of his claws the cougar shredded Roy's left boot. Leaping out of the saddle, he killed the cougar with his bare hands, threw the dead animal over the saddle, and returned angrily to the ranch house.

His ever-faithful wife, Dale, standing on the porch, immediately sized up the situation and exclaimed:

"Pardon me, Roy, is that the cat that chewed your new shoe?"

4. A tourist from Tel Aviv walked into an ornate chapel maintained by Vishnu Maharishi, an up-and-coming young New Delhi faith healer famous for his talkativeness. The Israeli visitor pointed at a gilt-edged bench in front of the chapel and asked a nearby attendant:

"Pardon me, goy, is this the chatty new guru's pew?"

5. On the set of a new *Thin Man* movie, a prop man

noticed Myrna Loy carrying a swatch of material in her hand. Said he:

"Pardon me, Loy, is that the shantung that's the new clue?"

6. Lamont Cranston, renowned crime fighter, was actually a secret candy-bar freak. One Saturday he went into his dressing room to satisfy the craving of his sweet tooth, and made a beeline toward his hidden cache of candy bars. There he espied his usually faithful Chinese manservant munching happily on something, and said with annoyance:

"Pardon me, Toy, is that the Shadow's nougat you chew?"

7. A new patient, one Mrs. L., was ushered into the office of Sigmund Freud in nineteenth-century Vienna. At first Mrs. L. was ill at ease in the presence of the great man, and extremely hesitant about explaining her troubles. Dr. Freud suggested that she lie down on the couch and say anything, whatever came into her head. Mrs. L., relaxing despite herself, started to talk, at first haltingly. Then, speaking compulsively, she found herself revealing her single greatest fear — that she was going crazy.

Suddenly, feeling terribly self-conscious, Mrs. L. stopped in midsentence, looked over at the great doctor, and said:

"Pardon me, Freud, but is my chatter really cuckoo?"

8. This one is so long it must be abbreviated: An unprecedented pan-Eastern dinner was held some years back which was hosted by Premier Chou of China and included Nguyen Van Thieu of Vietnam. After watching the Chinese leader put away one nut-and-spice dish after another, one of the leaders turned to the Vietnamese leader and asked,

"Pardon me, Nguy, how many cashews did our Chou chew?"

9. A man had a favorite hat which he had worn for many years. Recently, however, the brim had been loosened in an accident and the man had been obliged to effect repairs with glue. The day after he had fixed the hat, he had a lunch date with a friend at a Chinese restaurant and, since it was a cold day, he wore a hat. They were sitting at the table and the man had his hat in his lap when his friend accidentally spilled soy sauce across the table and onto the man's hat. The friend said,

"Pardon the soy, is that the hat you put the glue to?"

10. Not to be outdone by the "Snap, crackle, pop!" of the cereal industry, a confectionary chemist invented a candy that talks when you bite into it. So if you hear the words "Yummy, yummy slurp, slurp, I'm so good" coming from the mouth of a chomping youngster, you can ask,

"Pardon me, boy, is that the chatty nougat you chew?"

11. Don Pardo, the famous announcer of *Saturday Night Live* fame, became incensed by the continued exploitation of the endangered naugha, which is brutally hunted for its hide. First he formed "Friends of the Naugha" and then to demonstrate his love of the little beast decided to raise a spirited naugha pup as a pet. After several years of care and feeding he thought it might be a good idea to take it back to the vet who had originally examined it when it was a newborn. The vet took one look at the animal and exclaimed,

"Pardo, my boy, is this what the little naugha grew to?"

12. The maître d' at a fancy restaurant gets one whiff of the fish of the day and puts out the word that he is banning it because it has gone bad.

Later one of the busboys passes by with what appears

to be a half-eaten portion of the fish. He stops him and asks:

"Pardon me, boy, but is this the shad I meant to ta-boo?"

Here Come the Elephants

They first lumbered onto the scene in early 1963, building on prototypes which had been kicking around for years. ("What did Tarzan say when he saw the elephants?" "I don't know, what did Tarzan say?" "Here come the elephants.")

Time magazine immediately termed them ". . . an escape from an overlogical and overmechanical world." Later, in an article in the *Journal of Popular Culture*, they were said to have arrived "just in time to save a country which was up to its neck in earnestness and involvement, on the one hand, and wretched political satire . . . on the other." Perhaps.

Then as now, their appeal lay in large, relentless doses, and to tell just one or two is to miss the whole point. They also tend to work better if you happen to be between the ages of nine and fifteen. It was no fluke that the best of elephant-joke books — *101 Elephant Jokes* — was written by Robert Blake, fourteen, who ran the following warning at the beginning of his work: "Practically no parents will think elephant jokes are funny."

But all of this is quite irrelephant; bring on the jokes.

How much did the psychiatrist charge the elephant?
  Thirty-five dollars for the visit and $350 for the couch.

What is gray, has short antennae, large wings, a long
nose, and gives money to elephants?
The tusk fairy.

How do you get down from an elephant?
You don't get down from an elephant, you get
down from a goose.

Why do elephants live in the jungle?
Because it is out of the high-rent district.

What's the similarity between an elephant and a
grape?
They're both purple, except for the elephant.

Why do elephants drink?
They want to forget.

Why does an elephant have cracks between his toes?
To carry his library card.

What did the elephant do when he broke his toe?
He called a tow truck.

What did the grape say when the elephant stepped
on it?
Nothing, it just let out a little whine.

Why do elephants have wrinkled ankles?
They lace their sneakers too tightly.

What did the banana say to the elephant?
Nothing. Bananas can't talk.

Why don't elephants like martinis?
Have you ever tried to get an olive out of your
trunk?

How do you get an elephant out of a tub of Jell-O?
Follow the directions on the back of the box.

How can you prevent an elephant from charging?
Take away his credit card.

How do you make an elephant float?
   Take two scoops of ice cream, an elephant, and
   some root beer.

Why do elephants wear sneakers?
   To creep up on mice.

How can you tell if an elephant has been in your refrigerator?
   From the footprints in the butter.

What's the difference between an elephant and a jar
   of peanut butter?
   The elephant doesn't stick to the roof of your
   mouth.

Why do elephants have trunks?
   Because they don't have glove compartments.

What do you call it when an elephant sits on a
   fence?
   Time to buy a new fence.

Why did the elephant paint his toenails different
   colors?
   So he could hide in the M&M's.

What's gray on the inside and clear on the outside?
   A elephant in a Baggie.

What does an elephant call a dinosaur?
   Extinct.

What has two tails, six feet, and three trunks?
   An elephant with spare parts.

If there were three elephants in the kitchen, which
   one would be the cowboy?

The one on the range.

What weighs two thousand pounds and is covered
with lettuce and mayonnaise?
A Big McElephant.

Why are there no elephants in Hawaii?
Because they can't afford the air fare.

What do you do with an elephant with three balls?
Walk him and pitch to the giraffe.

What happens when you cross an elephant and a
prostitute?
A three-quarter-ton pickup.

Why did the elephant sit on the marshmallow?
So he wouldn't fall into the hot chocolate.

What do you get when you cross an elephant and a
mouse?
Dunno, but it sure makes big holes in the walls.

How do you get an elephant out of your bathtub?
Pull the plug.

What is gray and powdery?
Instant elephant.

What do you find between elephant's toes?
Slow-running pygmies.

What has twelve legs, is pink, and goes, "Bah, bah,
bah?"
Three pink elephants singing "The Whiffenpoof
Song."

What is gray and stamps out jungle fires?
Smokey the elephant.

What is Smokey the Elephant's middle name?
The.
What's convenient and weighs twelve hundred
pounds?

An elephant six-pack.

What did the drunk elephant say to the second
  drunk elephant?
  Don't look now, but is that a pink human?

How can you tell if there are elephants under your
  bed?
  You can touch the ceiling with your nose.

What's covered with fur, has a long trunk, and loves
  peanuts?
  An elephant in a mink coat.

What has big ears, weighs two thousand pounds, and
  has two trunks?
  An elephant going on vacation.

Why aren't elephants allowed on beaches?
  Because they can't keep their trunks up.

What weighs four thousand pounds and sings?
  Harry Elefonte.

What's black, covered with feathers, and weighs two
  thousand pounds?
  An elephant that's been tarred and feathered.

Why don't many elephants go to college?
  Few finish high school.

What's red on the outside and gray on the inside?
  Campbell's cream of elephant soup!

What happens to old elephant jokes?
  They fall flat.

Elephant jokes begat a string of like absurdities:

Banana Jokes

What do you call a banana in prison?
A convict.

What do cannibals eat for dessert?
Bawana splits.

Grape Jokes

What do you call great bodies of water filled with grape juice?
The Grape Lakes.

What's purple and goes buzz, buzz, buzz?
An electric grape.

What's the largest thing ever made of grapes?
The Grape Wall of China.

What's small, purple, and dangerous?
A grape with a submachine gun.

What's large, purple, and lies across the ocean?
Grape Britain.

Tomato Jokes

What's red and goes up and down, up and down?
A tomato in an elevator.

Why didn't the tomato go to the dentist?
Tomatoes don't have teeth.

How do you fix a broken tomato?
With tomato paste.

What's red, runs on batteries, and costs six million dollars?
The Bionic Tomato.

Plum Jokes

What noted plum wrote under an assumed name?
  Nom de Plum.

How do you tell a plum from an elephant?
  A plum always forgets.

What do you call an eight-hundred-pound plum with
  a nasty temper?
  Sir.

Gorilla Jokes

Why did the ape wear blue suspenders?
  His red ones broke.

What's the best way to call a mean gorilla?
  Long distance.

Monster Jokes

How does a monster count to fourteen?
  On his fingers.

What do sea monsters eat?
  Fish and ships.

How do you train King Kong?
  Hit him with a rolled-up newspaper building.

There is no end to all of this and anyone who thinks
this absurdist fad is over hasn't been within earshot of
a schoolyard in recent years.

Said Swiftly

They are, for lack of a better term, high-speed puns. Some of us love them for just that reason — no story, no buildup, just quick formulaic hits best delivered in relentless salvos. From a larger field here are five twentieth-century examples starting with a form, admittedly sexist by today's standards, which became popular in the 1920s and continued strong until the end of World War II.*

I

She Was Only a . . .

. . . artist's daughter, but what a crowd she could draw (or, . . . but she knew where to draw the line).

. . . attorney's daughter but what a will to break.

. . . blacksmith's daughter, but she knew how to forge ahead.

. . . bottlemaker's daughter, but nothing could stop her.

. . . boxer's daughter, but she knew when to faint.

---

*These were still popular in my neighborhood in the late 1940s and fully half of those listed here were dredged from the crevices of my brain, where they had been stored for all that time. When they started pouring forth I finally figured I may have failed geometry in the seventh grade because my brain was too cluttered with such things to make room for theorems.

. . . carnival queen, but she made a lot of concessions.

. . . censor's daughter, but she knew when to cut it out.

. . . chauffeur's daughter, but she could shift for herself.

. . . chimney sweep's daughter, but she soots me fine.

. . . coal dealer's daughter, but, oh, where she had bin.

. . . conductor's daughter, but she told you where to get off.

. . . convict's daughter, but she certainly knew all the bars.

. . . doctor's daughter, but she knew how to operate.

. . . electrician's daughter, but she went haywire.

. . . fruit-store owner's daughter, but, oh, what a peach.

. . . golfer's daughter, but her form was perfect.

. . . governor's daughter, but what a state she was in.

. . . hash slinger's daughter, but how she could dish it out.

. . . horseman's daughter, but she didn't know how to say nay.

. . . jockey's daughter, but all the horsemen knew her.

. . . judge's daughter, but she could dispose of any case.

. . . milkman's daughter, but she was the cream of the crop.

. . . minister's daughter, but you couldn't put anything past her.

. . . moonshiner's daughter, but I love her still.

. . . parson's daughter, but she had her following.

. . . poet's daughter, but I've seen verse.

. . . plumber's daughter, but, oh, those fixtures.

. . . prizefighter's daughter, but she certainly knew all the ropes.

. . . quarryman's daughter, but she took everything for granite.

. . . railroader's daughter, but her caboose was the talk of the town.

. . . realtor's daughter, but, oh, what development.

. . . sergeant's daughter, but she knew when to call a halt.

. . . shoemaker's daughter, but she gave the boys her awl and stuck to the last.

. . . surgeon's daughter, but oh what a cutup.

. . . taxi driver's daughter, but you auto meter.

. . . telephone operator's daughter, but she had good connections.

. . . waitress's daughter, but she sure could dish it out.

Daughters were finally eclipsed by:

II

Oldies

On April 19, 1951, General MacArthur delivered his farewell address to a joint session of Congress. As part of his farewell, he quoted a line from an old song — "Old soldiers never die, they just fade away" — and a new formula was born.

First came the puns:

General Dye retired and moved to a small seaside town called Faye, where he spent many hours wading in the surf. An old comrade visited him and came back to report to his friends, "Old Dye never soldiers, he just wades at Faye."

And then came these:

Old bathing beauties never die, they just wade away.

Old crapshooters never die, they just fade away.

Old gardeners never die, they just spade away.
Old hairdressers never die, they just braid away.
Old teachers never die, they just grade away.

Which, in turn, were followed by these:
Old accountants never die, they're just disfigured.
Old auctioneers never die, they just look forbidding.
Old ballplayers never die, they're just debased.
Old botanists never die, they're just deflowered.
Old cardiologists never die, they just lose heart.
Old committee members never die, they are just disappointed.
Old fishermen never die, they just smell that way.
Old generals never die, they are just debased.
Old helicopter pilots never die, they just lose their choppers.
Old housewives never die, they just wash away.
Old janitors never die, they just kick the bucket.
Old lawyers never die, they just lose their appeal.
Old mathematicians never die, they are just nonplussed.
Old orchestra leaders never die, they are just disbanded.
Old pickpockets never die, they just steal away.
Old poker players never die, they are just discarded.
Old postal workers never die, they just become unzipped.
Old railroad workers never die, they just get derailed.
Old sign painters never die, they just letter go.
Old songwriters never die, they just decompose.
Old tree surgeons never die, they are just uprooted.
Old washing machine operators never die, they just keep agitating.

This type of pun enjoys periodic, limited revival, although the exact format changes. A recent incarnation came in one of Elaine Viets's 1981 columns in the *St. Louis Post-Dispatch*. A reader sent her a quote by Virginia Ostman which appears in the book *Peter's Quotations* and asks,

If lawyers are disbarred and clergymen defrocked, doesn't it follow that electricians can be delighted; musicians denoted; cowboys deranged; models deposed; tree surgeons debarked and dry cleaners depressed?

Viets and her readers rose to the occasion and supplied a number of de- and dis- words for various professions. Here are some of those findings augmented by contributions from the fertile mind of Russell Dunn, Sr.

Bankers = discredited
Butchers = delivered
Caped crusaders = dismantled
Celebrities = defamed
Citizens = devoted
Curtain makers = depleted
Dentists = decayed
Detectives = dissolved
Fisherman = debated
Grammarian = denounced
Hair stylists = distressed
Magicians = disillusioned
Married women = dismissed
Mathematicians = deciphered
Moonshiners = disconcerted
Packers = desecrated
Photographers = developed
Pig farmers = disgruntled
Poker players = deduced
Preachers = decreed
Reporters = depressed
Sightseers = detoured
Sleepers = debunked
Songwriters = decomposed
Students = detested
Teachers = degraded
Telephone operators = disconnected
Vegetarians = decelerated
Weavers = defrayed

III

Adverbial Abuse

The premise was based on a quaint and obvious

mannerism used in the original Edward L. Stratemeyer Tom Swift books. This was to have an adverb match what Tom was saying. Although others had played with adverbial puns before, it was not until the early 1960s that it became a fad with a name. They were called Tom Swifties after three San Franciscans — Paul Pease, Bill McDonough, and John Larrecq — hit on the idea of a series of books which immortalized such lines as "What our ball club needs is a man who can hit sixty homers per season," said Tom ruthlessly, and "My commute ticket expired," said Tom extraneously.

As with all fads, the Tom Swiftie fad had its time; but to this day there are those who continue to collect and concoct adverbial puns. The collection assembled here (which also includes several *verbal* puns) contains, among others, more than a hundred from Mike Weber and Caroline Bryan of Milwaukee. (I'd mention the company they work for except that it looks as though they used the company's computer for this important work and it's possible this would make the company's other work look trivial by comparison.) Not only is this one of the longest lists of adverbial puns ever assembled, but because of the work of Weber and Bryan it is compiled alphabetically by adverb from "abashedly" through "wryly" — a major breakthrough for those who need a quick match for "high-handedly" or "vibrantly."

"I smashed up both my front fenders," she said abashedly.

"Nobody showed up," he replied absently.

"Okay, wise guy, I'll splash some on your clothes" was his acid reply.

"You will pay for eating that apple," God said adamantly.

"And fifteen more baseball gloves," he admitted.

"I will let you in without a ticket," he admitted.

"I can't think of any more poetry," she said adversely.

"Uh-oh, I'm out of fuel," said he aghast.

"But who is flying this airplane?" he asked airily.

"Let's buy some of that fresh fruit," she said with aplomb.

"Is that a Picasso?" he asked artfully.

"They just stole all my paintings," she said artlessly.

"Yes, I'll buy that perfume," he assented.

"I'm trying to do something about my bad breath," he asserted.

"No, officer, I was sitting here on my backside," he asserted.

"I must judge how well he cut the donkey loose," he asseverated.

"I am Lord High Executioner of the guillotine," he asseverated.

"This exam is the toughest of the year," he attested.

"Yes, you may copy from the book I wrote," he authorized.

"This is power steering," he said automatically.

"You, my friend, are losing your hair," he stated baldly.

"Yes, I'm starring in a French movie," she barely blurted out.

"Feed your dog," his father barked.

"Ulp, I just swallowed a fish lure," said he with bated breath.

"I'm glad you got your headlight fixed," she beamed.

"Blow on the fire and it will burn better," he bellowed.

"Fan that fire faster!" the blacksmith bellowed.

"Somebody forgot the sugar in the lemonade," she complained bitterly.

"My bed isn't made," he complained in a blanket statement.

"I am awfully sunburned" was her blistering remark.

"What? Fly into this hurricane?" he cried breezily.

"Where is the lamp?" he asked brightly.

"See my new camera?" he asked candidly.

"Let's send these packages to the poor overseas," she said carefully.

"This acid will *really* clean your silverware," she replied caustically.

"Household tasks can be fun," he chortled.

"Right this way, Charles," she chuckled.

"I have just washed all your windows," he spoke out clearly.

"Which of these @#%&* classes should I take?" he asked coarsely.

"C'mon, have another soda," he coaxed.

"I haven't started painting yet," he remarked colorlessly.

"She flew with us," she complained.

"Take the prisoner below," said the captain condescendingly.

"I did it with the actor Mr. Parker," she confessed.

"Our sockets are overloaded," she declared confusedly.

"I am going to join the Trappists," he said contemplatively.

"We've reached the South Pole," he remarked coolly.

"But I do not know Mr. Geiger," he countered.

"Do you play golf?" he would ask as a matter of course.

"Will you marry me?" he asked with courtly gestures.

"I'm going to stay away from the Brahma bull," the rider said, cowed.

"I've dropped my toothpaste," he stated crestfallen.

"Let's begin the operation," the doctor said cuttingly.

"I can't see in this closet," he hinted darkly.

"That will be four hundred dollars," the mortician said with deadly precision.

"I had a flat tire," he said somewhat deflatedly.

"The horse just shrugged and he fell right off," she derided.

"This is the Venus de Milo," the guide said disarmingly.

"I did my best to take the puzzle apart," he dissembled.

"Delilah has cut my hair!" said Samson, somewhat distressed.

"Well, I'll be an SOB," he said doggedly.

"Watch out for that hive in the tree," she droned.

"There's too much vermouth in my martini," she said dryly.

"Piece o' cake," she replied effortlessly.

"Do you think I needed all those vitamins?" he asked energetically.

"I accept your proposal," she replied engagingly.

"Stay away from that precious ancient urn," she pleaded evasively.

"Yes, father, we lost our mine to that prospector," she exclaimed.

"That dessert will destroy my diet," she expanded richly.

"I just flew in from the Coast," he explained.

"There's sixteen ounces in that bag," she expounded.

"Hey, watch where you're going on the turnpike!" he shouted expressly.

"I feel dizzy," she whispered faintly.

"I feel so good after going to church," she said faithfully.

"Take my temperature," he said feverishly.

"I always salute the Stars and Stripes," he bragged flagrantly.

"Columbus will fall off the edge of the earth," he said flatly.

"Uh-oh, a blowout," he said flatly.

"It's the Navy," he said fleetingly.

"Is the tumbling act still in town?" he asked flippantly.

"Let's play tiddledywinks," she said flippantly.

"What good is French money?" she asked frankly.

"My wallet fell out during the dance," he said frugally.

"We are going to have a record harvest this year," he said fruitfully.

"I smell gas," he fumed.

"Do you play tennis?" he asked gamely.
"I hope we bag a rhino," he said gamely.
"I'll see if I can dig it up," he said gravely.
"Look out for the bear," he yelled in a grisly voice.
"No one gets past this gate," the officer said guardedly.

"They have stabbed me through," she said halfheartedly.
"Well, I'm not exactly finished trimming the bushes," she hedged.
"Please, teacher, may I leave the room?" she asked high-handedly.
"I've won the daily double," he cried hoarsely.
"We will burn your embassy," they cried hotly.
"And tear down the Stars and Stripes," they said unflaggingly.

"Alter your course: glacier up ahead!" he responded icily.
"Nobody wants my services anymore," the doctor said impatiently.
"This is the chicken-pox ward," the nurse said infectiously.
"I just adore this new mink coat," she inferred.
"I don't have a penny to my name," he said innocently.
"She's my parents' daughter," he insisted.
"You know, this magnet really works!" he said ironically.
"Oh, that crummy poison ivy," she said irritably.

"I've lost my rare Chinese brooch," she said jadedly.

"When can I take this cast off?" he asked lamely.
"The plumbing in the White House needs repair," the reporters leaked.
"No, sir, there are no hills in this road," said the gas station attendant on the level.

"Let us all raise our champagne in a toast," she said with lifted spirits.

"Then you suck this hose from the helium tank," he said light-headedly.

"They ain't gonna take me alive," said Long John Silver limply.

"Uh-oh, I forgot what to get at the store," he said listlessly.

"I wish I were taller," she said longingly.

"This coat is at least two sizes too large," she said loosely.

"I'm the janitor around here," he maintained.

"Put prices on all merchandise," he said markedly.

"So many aggies and cat's-eyes in the deluxe set!" he marveled.

"I must get back to the store," she said, minding her own business.

"I can't milk this cow," he said moodily.

"Very talkative cats you have there, ma'am," he mused.

"Where will I get inspiration for my ode?" she mused.

"I'll get even with that lousy hound," he muttered.

"We hung out our flag on the Fourth of July," he observed.

"Hey, watch where you're cutting," he said off-handedly.

"I'd say your pants are too short," the tailor said off the cuff.

"It's a nice Christmas tree," she opined.

"What a rotten hand you've dealt me," said the bridge player in passing.

"Are you a doctor?" she asked patiently.

"What vegetable goes with carrots?" she asked peacefully.

"I get Time, Newsweek, and U.S. News," he would say periodically.

"Better brush your shoes clean," he persuaded.

"Darling daughter, you've been on the phone for an hour," he said phonetically.

"I'm taking harp lessons," the student said pluckily.

"Get that pin off my chair," she demanded pointedly.

"This will break our budget," he explained poorly.

"All our rooms are filled, sir," said the clerk with a preoccupied air.

"Hello, class, I am your teacher," she professed.

"Psst! Your next line is on the cue card," he said promptly.

"Isn't that a peculiar reaction?" the scientist queried.

"Stop! I'm alive," she yelled quickly.

"Get out of these headwaters," he cried rapidly.

"It's the measles," the doctor diagnosed rashly.

"That mirror was a real good investment," he said upon reflection.

"Sorry, we can't pick up your garbage," he refused.

"Oh, no, my mother-in-law is coming," he said, relatively annoyed.

"I had to regrade those essays," she remarked.

"I didn't really send that telegram twice, did I?" she cried remorsefully.

"I have to glue these sheets of wood back together," he replied.

"The chorus must sing again," she required.

"The only other lodge is a hundred miles from here," said he as a last resort.

"Fishing and swimming in the summer, skating in the winter," he responded.

"We're going to have leftover cutlets tonight," she revealed.

"Stop the music!" he rhapsodized.

"I'll hit you with my best punch," he said righteously.

"Hey, I'm weightless," said the astronaut, rising to the occasion.

"Our carpet has really taken a lot of wear," she said ruggedly.

"There are twelve inches in a foot," the judge ruled.

"This tractor is quite weather-beaten," he said rustically.

"My dear wife has left me," he cried ruthlessly.

"There's a lot of cactus on this prairie," she observed sagely.

"Yes, dear, I always have hollandaise on potatoes," she said saucily.

"Get your hands off the oven," she screamed scorchingly.

"I'll have to look for it," he replied searchingly.

"We've just survived another earthquake," she said, visibly shaken.

"I broke your glasses" was her shattering statement.

"This wool *is* pretty low quality," she said sheepishly.

"How do you like my petticoat?" she asked shiftlessly.

"I can't find my glasses," he said shortsightedly.

"Honey, will you *please* stop nagging me?" he asked shrewdly.

"Do you want laughing gas while I drill?" the dentist asked smilingly.

"You've mussed my hair!" she snarled.

"This is pretty bad candy," she snickered.

"You've got a pretty big nose," he said snootily.

"He stabbed me through," he said sordidly.

"Aha, but you have signed your afterlife away," the devil said soulfully.

"The price for these lemons is ridiculous," she said sourly.

"You'll need this for your bike wheel," he spoke.

"We try to keep our Christmas trees fresh," he said sprucing up.

"We're about to run out of gas," he sputtered.

"Ug. You-um be Thunder Cloud's wife," he squawked.

"Alabama, Alaska, Arizona, Arkansas . . ." she stated.

"Pipe down," the steam fitter shouted.

"Let's stay ahead of the other boat," the captain said sternly.

"I can't help laughing over my operation," said he in stitches.

"There is too much starch in this shirt," he said stiffly.

"What's that bird with the long beak?" the little girl asked stoically.

"Rats, it's going to rain again today," he stormed.

"The house is right up ahead," he said straightforwardly.

"That tree trunk wasn't there last night," she said, stumped.

"So for homework, learn these arithmetic tables," the teacher summed up.

"I am going to keep all my money," he surmised.

"I have just sat on some upholstery nails," he said tactfully.

"I don't *have* to do this for a living," she said tartly.

"Call me a cab!" he bellowed taxingly.

"The revenue people are after me again," he replied taxingly.

"My dentures nearly fell off the cliff," she said with teeth on edge.

"You gave me two less than a dozen," he said tensely.

"I've got a lot of things on my mind," she asserted thoughtfully.

"Yes, we're going to have an earthquake," he averred with a tremor.

"See my new sports car?" he asked triumphantly.

"We can form a monopoly with this merger," they declared trustingly.

"But I *do* work in a pretzel factory," he thought in his twisted mind.

"Don't tell me I'm out of hash," he growled uncannily.

"This plane is about to crash!" he sobbed uncontrollably.

"I got all D's on my exams," she would cry unfailingly.

"My hand is numb," she said unfeelingly.

"Sorry, there is no guarantee with this one," was the unwarranted reply.

"I am insane," he said unwittingly.

"You must be Kareem Abdul-Jabbar," he spoke up.

"Aw, go milk a cow," she uttered.

"I see Dudley cut classes again," she commented vacantly.

"Quit feeling my pulse!" he shouted in vain.

"I have just learned to play the xylophone," he said vibrantly.

"But I've always lived just west of England," he wailed.

"Here is the fourth Timex I have found this week," she said watchfully.

"Oh, how I hate long good-byes," she wavered.

"Our paper comes out four times a month," he said weakly.

"Aren't five cups from one tea bag too much?" she asked weakly.

"I'm glad I did well on my EKG," he said wholeheartedly.

"You won't get a penny from me when I die," he said willfully.

"My horse won't stop," he shouted woefully.

"I can't imagine what happened to those loaves of bread," he wondered.

"What kind of bread should I bake?" the baker asked wryly.

IV
Do Its

The most recent outbreak of the disease caused by the same virus that brought on the Tom Swiftie epidemic has come in the form of "do its." It all started with a few T-shirts and bumper stickers proclaiming such truths as: "Nurses do it with patience," and "Teachers do it with class." They proliferated and the highways were soon turned into a forum for professional/sexual puns. No matter that some were forced — "Dancers do it with their feet," and "Potters do it with clay" don't exactly cater to mainstream fantasies — the fad has created some great bumper-to-bumper reading.

The nation's leading collector/creator of "do its" is Dr. Reinhold Aman, editor of *Maledicta: The International Journal of Verbal Aggression.* Aman has collected enough to have published a book of them (available from Maledicta Press, 331 South Greenfield Avenue, Waukesha, Wisconsin 53186). Here is a small selection from his much larger recollection:

Admirals do it fleetingly.
Anesthesiologists do it unconsciously.
Artisans do it craftily.

Bankers do it interestingly.
Beginners do it startingly.
Belgians do it bilingually.
Ben does it gaily.
Bigots do it intolerably.

Californians do it sharingly.
Camels do it humpingly.
Cannoneers do it ballistically.
Canoeists do it with their paddles.
Cardiologists do it heartily.
Catholics do it rhythmically.

Chicagoans do it breezily.
Chinese do it inscrutably.
City slickers do it urbanely.
Clockmakers do it watchfully.
Columnists do it regularly.
Compulsives do it neatly.
Computer operators do it bit.by bit.

Defense attorneys do it objectingly.
Dentists do it inextricably.
Dermatologists do it flakily.
Dogs do it cynically.
Dolphins do it flippantly.
Donkeys do it asininely.
Drill operators do it boringly.
Drinkers do it spiritually.
Drummers do it differently.

Editors do it grumpily.
Einstein did it relatively.
Electronics engineers do it unbiasedly.
Elephants do it with their trunk.
Emperors do it majestically.
Engineers do it mechanically.
Eunuchs do it uniquely.
Exhibitionists do it flashily.
Experts do it authoritatively.

Felines do it cattily.
Field marshals do it strategically.
Frankenstein did it monstrously.
Frenchmen do it frankly.

Germans do it markedly.
Gibbons do it swingingly.
Gillespie does it dizzily.
Grammarians do it punctually.
Gregory did it enchantingly.

Hairdressers do it permanently.
Helen does it readily.

Henry did it thoroughly.
Hotheads do it quickly.

Illiterates do it indescribably.
Indian guides do it unerringly.
Ivan did it terribly.

Jacob and Wilhelm did it grimly.
Johnny Carson does it four times a week.
Journalists do it reportedly.

King Arthur did it nightly.
Knights do it boldly.

Lawbreakers do it offensively.
Lensmakers do it objectively.
Libertines do it freely.
Louisianans do it bayoutifully.

Magicians do it inexplicably.
Mailmen do it zippingly.
Masturbators do it singlehandedly.
Mathematicians do it figuratively.
Michelangelo did it on his back.
Miners do it with their shaft.
Monoglots do it unilingually.
Motorists do it exhaustingly.
Mountaineers do it condescendingly.
Musicians do it harmonically.
Myopics do it shortsightedly.

Nouveaux riches do it upwardly.
Nudists do it barely.

Oil refinery workers do it crudely.
Omahans do it mutually.

Paranoids do it suspiciously.
Painters do it with even strokes.
Philosophers do it questionably.
Pigs do it sloppily.
Poles do it with polish.
Printers do it without wrinkling the sheets.

Procrastinators do it later.
Professors do it testily.
Prostitutes do it tartly.

Rabbits do it hairily.
Railroad engineers do it tenderly.
Reporters do it sensationally.
Roosters do it cockily
Rulers do it measuredly.

San Franciscans do it shakily.
Schizophrenics do it twice.
Semioticians do it symbolically.
Septuagenarians do it weakly weekly.
Shriners do it conventionally.
Skeptics do it incredibly.
Spies do it under cover.
Statisticians do it averagely.
Studs do it polysemously.
Sycophants do it praisingly.

Tautologists do it repeatedly.
Thespians do it playfully.
Thieves do it stealthily.
Tom does it swiftly.
Triplets do it thrice.
Truckers do it wrecklessly.
Trumpeters do it hornily.
Twins do it doubly.

Undertakers do it gravely.

Venus de Milo did it unarmedly.
Violinists do it unstrungly.

Wagnalls does it funkily.
Washingtonians do it diplomatically.
Whores do it trickily.
Widows do it lamentably.
Witch doctors do it charmingly.
Writers do it literally.

Operknockety Tunes

In the early days the vast majority of knock-knocks were lines from songs, which meant you got to sing the fifth line. To some purists these are to be considered a separate art form and should never be mixed with the stated types. Here, then, is a separate hoard, many of which date back to the Big Band Era.

Knock, Knock.
Who's there?
Aardvark.
Aardvark who?
Aardvark a million miles for one of your smiles.

Knock, Knock.
Who's there?
Agatha.
Agatha who?
Agatha world on a string.

Knock, Knock.
Who's there?
Akron.
Akron who?
Akron give you anything but love, baby.

Knock, Knock.
Who's there?

Amahl.
Amahl who?
Amahl shook up.

Knock, Knock.
Who's there?
Ammonia.
Ammonia who?
Ammonia bird in a gilded cage.

Knock, Knock.
Who's there?
Annie.
Annie who?
Annie thing you can do, I can do better.

Knock, Knock.
Who's there?
Apocryphal.
Apocryphal who?
I've got Apocryphal of dreams.

Knock, Knock.
Who's there?
Barrymore.
Barrymore who?
Barrymore not on the lone prairie.

Knock, Knock.
Who's there?
Barton.
Barton who?
Barton up your overcoat.

Knock, Knock.
Who's there?
Bay.

Bay who?
Bay be face, you've got the cutest little baby face.

Knock, Knock.
Who's there?
Barry.
Barry who?
Barry me not on the lone prairie.

Knock, Knock.
Who's there?
Big Horse.
Big Horse who?
Big Horse of you.

Knock, Knock.
Who's there?
Caesar.
Caesar who?
Caesar jolly good fellow, Caesar jolly good fellow.

Knock, Knock.
Who's there?
Crimea.
Crimea who?
Crimea river. I cried a river over you.

Knock, Knock.
Who's there?
Darrell.
Darrell who?
Darrell never be another you.

Knock, Knock.
Who's there?
Deirdre.
Deirdre who?

Deirdre mother come from Ireland?

Knock, Knock.
Who's there?
Dexter.
Dexter who?
Dexter halls with boughs of holly.

Knock, Knock.
Who's there?
Domino.
Domino who?
Domino thing if you ain't got that swing.

Knock, Knock.
Who's there?
Domino.
Domino who?
Domino cowhand.

Knock, Knock.
Who's there?
Don Ameche.
Don Ameche who?
I'll be Don Ameche in a taxi, honey.

Knock, Knock.
Who's there?
Don Juan.
Don Juan who?
I Don Juan to set the world on fire.

Knock, Knock.
Who's there?
Donna.
Donna who?
Donna sit under the apple tree.

Knock, Knock.
Who's there?
Ferry.
Ferry who?
Ferry tales can come true.

Knock, Knock.
Who's there?
Frankfurter.
Frankfurter who?
Frankfurter memories.

Knock, Knock.
Who's there?
Freeze.
Freeze who?
Freeze a jolly good fellow.

Knock, Knock.
Who's there?
Gnome.
Gnome who?
Gnomebody knows the trouble I've seen.

Knock, Knock.
Who's there?
Greta.
Greta who?
Greta long, little dogie, greta long.

Knock, Knock.
Who's there?
Hal.
Hal who?
Hallelujah! I'm a bum.

Knock, Knock.
Who's there?

Heifer.
Heifer who?
If Heifer I should lose you.

Knock, Knock.
Who's there?
Humus.
Humus who?
Humus remember this, a kiss is just a kiss.

Knock, Knock.
Who's there?
Hyman.
Hyman who?
Hyman the mood for love.

Knock, Knock.
Who's there?
Igloo.
Igloo who?
Igloo Susie like I knew Susie.

Knock, Knock.
Who's there?
Ivy League.
Ivy League who?
Ivy League for every drop of rain that falls, a flower grows.

Knock, Knock.
Who's there?
Jimmy.
Jimmy who?
Jimmy that old time religion.

Knock, Knock.
Who's there?

Jose.
Jose who?
Jose can you see by the dawn's early light?
(This can also be accomplished with O'Shea.)

Knock, Knock.
Who's there?
Karloff.
Karloff who?
Karloff my dreams, I love you.

Knock, Knock.
Who's there?
Keir Dullea.
Keir Dullea who?
On a Keir Dullea you can see forever.
(Ina Claire was used in earlier versions.)

Knock, Knock.
Who's there?
Kelly.
Kelly who?
Kellyfornia, here I come!

Knock, Knock.
Who's there?
King Kong.
King Kong who?
King Kong the witch is dead.

Knock, Knock.
Who's there?
Lima Bean.
Lima Bean who?
Lima Bean working on the railroad.

Knock, Knock.
Who's there?

Llama.
Llama who?
Llama Yankee doodle dandy.

Knock, Knock.
Who's there?
Marcus Welby.
Marcus Welby who?
It Marcus Welby spring.

Knock, Knock.
Who's there?
Mary Lee.
Mary Lee who?
Mary Lee we roll along.

Knock, Knock.
Who's there?
Mean Tummy.
Mean Tummy who?
Why must you be Mean Tummy?

Knock, Knock.
Who's there?
Offenbach.
Offenbach who?
I have Offenbach on this street before.

Knock, Knock.
Who's there?
Oil Can.
Oil Can who?
My Oil Can Tuckey home.

Knock, Knock.
Who's there?
Olaf.

Olaf who?
Olaf my heart in San Francisco.

Knock, Knock.
Who's there?
Pettygil.
Pettygil who?
A Pettygil is like a melody.

Knock, Knock.
Who's there?
Picasso.
Picasso who?
Picasso you there's a song in my heart.

Knock, Knock.
Who's there?
Piranha.
Piranha who?
Piranha old gray bonnet . . .

Knock, Knock.
Who's there?
Sam and Janet.
Sam and Janet who?
Sam and Janet evening.

Knock, Knock.
Who's there?
Rapunzel.
Rapunzel who?
Rapunzel your troubles in your old kit bag.

Knock, Knock.
Who's there?
Shelby.
Shelby who?

Shelby coming around the mountain when she comes.

Knock, Knock.
Who's there?
Somber.
Somber who?
Somber over the rainbow.

Knock, Knock.
Who's there?
Sonia.
Sonia who?
Sonia shanty in ol' shanty town.

Knock, Knock.
Who's there?
Sony.
Sony who?
Sony a paper moon.

Knock, Knock.
Who's there?
Swedish.
Swedish who?
Ida, Swedish apple cider.

Knock, Knock.
Who's there?
Tarzan.
Tarzan who?
Tarzan Stripes forever.

Knock, Knock.
Who's there?
Theresa.
Theresa who?
Theresa nothing like a dame.

Knock, Knock.
Who's there?
Underwear.
Underwear who?
Underwear my baby is tonight?

Knock, Knock.
Who's there?
Venue.
Venue who?
Venue wish upon a star.

Knock, Knock.
Who's there?
Wendy.
Wendy who?
Wendy moon comes over the mountain.

Knock, Knock.
Who's there?
Yule.
Yule who?
Yule never know how much I love you.

Shaggy Dog Show

They are very hard to categorize. In his important *Esquire* essay on the subject J. C. Furnas concluded that "shaggy dog" is the only label that fits—*goofy*, for instance, is too broad, while *pointless* is too derogatory. Although he had no label for them, Furnas was able to describe the best of them as ". . . classics which, once heard, stick in the mind like taffy in a dog's jaw and are beautifully calculated to outrage people who can see nothing funny in them at all." Bennett Cerf, another shaggy dog expert, was content to define them by example: ". . . tales in which animals talk, humans do inexplicable things, and the punch line makes no sense at all."

But if they are hard to label, they are a delight to tell. Eric Partridge, the great expert on the English language, actually wrote a book entitled *The Shaggy Dog Story*, in which this point is made as well as it will ever be.

> The "shaggy dog" story does indeed represent the acme of the storyteller's art, for it demands a wittily unexpected and sudden ending, all the more unexpected in that the "lead-in" and the "lead-up" have had to be deceptively leisurely and almost diffuse; it demands also a considerable skill in narrative. . . . However absurd it may be, a "shaggy dog" must never be silly.

Although they have been divided in other ways, I am convinced that they fall into three natural categories: (1) stories about animals, (2) stories not about animals, and (3) stories about animals in bars.

In order to get as many of these as possible into the pages ahead, I have tightened them some. So when they are retold, you may want to embellish them a little to give them that "deceptively leisurely" quality which Partridge mentioned.

Also, there are two rules which should be observed when telling them: (1) Never say in advance that you are going to tell a shaggy dog story, as this will detract from the absurdity of it all, and (2) animals at bars almost always order martinis and the only other acceptable animal drink is a Manhattan. No other form of life, not even a parrot, would ever order a strawberry daiquiri.

1. Stories About Animals

This, according to Bennett Cerf and a number of others, was the prototypical tale first told in the early 1940s.

During the Great Depression a recently unemployed man in New York sat on a park bench, idly scanning a copy of the London *Times*. His eye fell upon an elegantly set advertisement for a lost shaggy dog, promising a "substantial reward." Shortly afterward he saw just such a dog, an Old English sheepdog, and collared it. Despite his dwindling resources, he bought a steamship ticket for himself, and a space for the dog, on a fast ocean liner, sailed for Southampton with anticipation, put dog and himself into a London train, and finally took a taxi to the Belgravia address shown in the ad. With the dog sitting beside him on the front steps, he rang the doorbell. After an appropriate pause the door opened, disclosing a butler in full regalia. Our hero said, "You advertised, I believe, for a lost shaggy dog." The butler looked down at the dog disdainfully, and remarked, "But not so shaggy as that, sir." He then closed the door.

Here, on the other hand, is a recent example of the art:

A traveler was driving through Arkansas when he lost his way and got off the main highway. In a short time he found himself driving along a narrow, bumpy back-country road.

Just as he began to wonder whether he should turn back or drive on until he could find a place to ask directions, he crested a hill, and in the valley beyond was the biggest pig farm he had ever seen.

As he drove by, he saw rows and rows of pigsties and pigpens, and pigs running in fields and pigs wallowing in mud. Suddenly his eye caught something really strange. He did a double take, muttered to himself, and then looked a third time. He wondered if he had seen correctly—it looked like a pig with a wooden leg!

He found the lane and drove up into the farmyard, where he was met by the farmer. "Excuse me," the traveler said. "I was just driving by and looking at all your pigs and everything, and I noticed something that I thought I just had to stop and ask about. Tell me, did I see right? Is there really a pig out there with a wooden leg?"

The farmer smiled. "Oh, that would be old Caesar you were seeing. He's the finest pig a man could ever hope to have—and smart! Well, let me tell you a little about that pig.

"You see that barge down there on the river? That's a mining dredge, taking out platinum ore. Old Caesar sniffed out the vein and showed us how to set it up. Now that dredge brings me in about a hundred and twenty thousand dollars every year.

"Over there in the meadow, you see those oil derricks? It was Caesar who showed them where to drill. Of course, it is just a small operation, but I got a quarter of a million on the mineral lease, and each year the wells bring me in about eighty thousand in royalties. See, I had Caesar negotiate the contract.

"Now, I can tell you are a city fellow, and you probably never thought of pigs as being particularly smart, much less intellectual, but old Caesar there, well, he has an honorary degree from the Sorbonne in Paris. Four or five times each year Caesar travels off to various universities both here and abroad to give guest lectures on theoretical physics. The honoraria from those lectures bring me twenty or twenty-five thousand every year, plus it is good advertising for the farm.

"There's another thing, a little more personal. One night a couple of years ago I got to drinking, and I guess I had more than I should have. I passed out drunk, fell down, and knocked over a lamp. That started a fire in the house, and old Caesar smelled the smoke. He came in the back door, got the wife and kid out, roused me up, and got me out. There is no question about it—that night old Caesar saved all our lives, and you know, that is not the sort of thing a man is going to forget too easily."

"Why," the traveler said, "this is all amazing! I have never heard of a pig like this before! This is fantastic! But tell me, how did he get that wooden leg? Was he in a wreck or something?"

The farmer laughed. "Well, naturally," he said, "when you have a pig that smart, you don't want to eat him all at one time."

A violinist believes that his music has become so captivating that he can now march into the deepest jungle and tame savage beasts by playing for them. He heads into the jungle and the first thing that happens is that two lions are entranced by his playing of Mozart. A panther and a leopard draw close and join the audience. Suddenly a hyena comes crashing through the underbrush, pounces on the violinist, and devours him, to the annoyance of the other animals.

"Why did you do a thing like that?" one of the lions says. "This man's music was magnificent, and just as we were really beginning to enjoy ourselves more than we have ever enjoyed ourselves before, you crash in here and destroy everything."

The hyena cups his paw to his ear, leans over closely to the lion and shouts, "What say?"

One goldfish to his tankmate: "If there's no God, who changes the water?"

An ad appears in the paper asking for an individual who can type, take dictation, program a computer, and speak more than one language.

The first applicant for the job is a dog. The dog is able to type at 145 words per minute, takes perfect dictation, and not only can program a computer but has written several programming manuals.

The prospective employer has the dog demonstrate all of these skills and then turns to him and says, "I'm dazzled by your qualifications, so I only have one final question: what about the language requirement?"

The dog looks at him and says, "Meow!"

All but one of a prized flock of homing pigeons return to their coop, and the owner becomes very worried.

At three in the morning the pigeon's owner is pacing the floor when he hears a tapping at the door. He opens it to find his lost bird, wet and bedraggled.

"What happened to you?" says the man.

"Well," replies the pigeon, "it was such a nice day I decided to walk."

"I have the greatest dog act," says the agent to the manager of a famous symphony hall.

"This isn't a circus," replies the manager.

"No, no, you don't understand. Bring the full orchestra into the hall and have the grand piano at center stage."

Reluctantly it is done and the agent then walks onto the stage with a small dog, who sits down and starts to play Grieg's Piano Concerto, flawlessly.

"This is the greatest thing I've ever seen," whispers the manager to the agent.

At that very moment a larger dog strides onto the stage.

"Is that dog also in the act?"

"No," replies the agent. "It's the dog's mother. She wanted him to be a doctor."

Years ago when the Dodgers were still in Brooklyn and Leo Durocher was the team's manager, a horse wandered up to the great manager and said, "Why don't you use me on your team, Leo? I can hit and field as well as anyone on your team."

"Get lost! I've got enough troubles."

"Come on, Leo, give me a chance—try me in the field."

"Okay, just for laughs."

The horse went into the field and made one spectacular catch after another.

"Amazing," said Durocher. "Come on in and bat."

The horse hit one ball after another over the fence and Durocher signed the horse on the spot.

The next day the Dodgers were playing the Giants. The first three Giants were put out by the dazzling fielding of the horse. The Dodgers came to bat and the first three men reached base. With the bases loaded the horse came to bat and he blasted the first ball over the Ebbets Field wall.

"Run, run!" Durocher yelled, but the horse just stood there.

"Are you kidding?" said the horse. "If I could run, I'd be racing at Jamaica!"

"Carry your bag?" said the redcap to the alligator about to board the plane for London.

"Sure, but be careful, that's my wife."

Two trained seals meet in their agent's outer office.

"It's terrible," said one. "Did you hear what happened to our old friend Fred?"

"What could it be? I heard that he finally got a job."

"That was the problem. He went to his first rehearsal, jumped in the tank, sank to bottom, and drowned. He'd been out of work so long he forgot how to swim."

A man is offered a magnificent horse at a very cheap price.

"What's wrong with him?" says the prospective buyer.

"Well, he has a strange habit. He sits down on grapefruit."

"I can live with that," says the buyer. "I'll take him."

A few hours later the buyer returns on foot. "I can't figure it out. I was riding across a stream and the horse sat down and still refuses to get up. I went into the water and felt around and couldn't find any grapefruit."

"Oh," says the seller, "I forgot to tell you he also sits down on fish."

"Somebody ate my porridge," bellowed Papa Bear.

"Somebody ate my porridge," cried Baby Bear.

"Oh, shut up," snapped Mama Bear. "I haven't even served it yet."

The actor entered the posh Beverly Hills restaurant with his pet terrier, asked for a table for two, and had the dog seated in the other chair. When the waiter handed the actor the menu, he became infuriated.

"Does it look like I'm eating alone?" he asked icily. "Service for two."

The dog was brought a menu and a full table setting and the two enjoyed a long, leisurely dinner.

After coffee and brandy, the waiter brought the check and placed it in front of the actor.

"How dare you?" yelled the actor, throwing the check on the table. "Don't you understand anything? I'm the guest."

The electric eel in the aquarium became depressed and his keeper asked if there was anything that could be done.

"I'm unhappy because I have no wife," said the eel.

The next day the keeper dropped a female eel into the tank, returned an hour later, and was shocked to find the male eel just as depressed as he had been before.

"What's the matter now?" he asked.

"Damn it," he said turning toward the intended mate, "DC."

Smith and Jones are on safari and one night after dinner Smith bets Jones a dollar that he will be the first to shoot a lion.

"In fact," says Smith. "I'll do it right now." Smith heads off into the jungle.

An hour later a lion pokes his head inside the tent and says, "You know a guy named Smith?"

Trembling, Jones says, "Well, yes."

"He owes you a dollar."

A young American doctor saved a baby elephant's life while traveling through the African jungle. Many years later the doctor finds himself in the most unenviable position: penniless, lost, and without a practice. One day he drifts into a small town, works for a few hours, and makes enough money to buy a drink and a cheap ticket to the circus, which is in town.

At the beginning of the circus the elephants come out. The lead elephant recognizes the old doctor and trumpets his joy at seeing him. Without hesitation he wraps his trunk around the doctor, lifts him out of his two-dollar seat and plunks him down on one of the five-dollar seats.

A female zebra working as a reporter is traveling around the U.S. for a report she is doing on the status of American animals.

She runs into a stallion on a country road, pulls out her notebook, and asks, "And what is it that you do, sir?"

The stallion says, "Lady, take off those silly pajamas and I'll show you."

Two dachshunds were chatting.

"I can't figure it out," said the first dog. "I'm in perfect physical shape but I'm constantly anxious."

"Why don't you go to a psychiatrist?" said the second.

"How can I? I'm not allowed on the couch."

A man buys a talking bird for his wife's birthday. It speaks seven languages and costs him a thousand dollars.

"Well, did you get the bird I sent you?" he asks that evening.

"Yes," says his wife. "I already have it in the oven."

"What! That bird could speak seven languages!"

"Then why didn't it say something?"

A missionary is chased through the jungle by a ferocious lion, who corners him. With no other option left, the missionary falls to his knees in prayer. To his great surprise the lion also begins to pray.

"This is miraculous," says the missionary, "joining me in prayer when I had given myself up for lost."

"Don't interrupt," says the lion, "I'm saying grace."

Two horses, followed by the stable dog, are on their way to the starting gate.

Says one, "Pal, we've been stablemates for the last five years. Today is my last race, as I will retire tomorrow and become a stud. I know you're the favorite, but maybe you could let me win this one, as it will improve my possibilities as a stud."

Just then the little dog blurts out, "Aha, I've heard every word of this shameful proposition and I'm going to report both of you to the trainer."

The second horse looks at the first horse and says, "Look, a talking dog!"

A traveling salesman arrives in a country store where he finds four men playing poker with a fox terrier. He becomes more amazed when he watches the dog call for two cards, raise his bet, and rake in the pot.

Finally he says, "That's amazing. I've never seen such a smart dog."

"He ain't smart," says one of the men at the table. "Whenever he gets a real good hand he wags his tail."

A man with a dog act went into a booking office. He had a Spitz and a fox terrier. The terrier would announce the act and tell jokes for a few minutes. The booking agent jumped up and said, "Wow, that terrier is terrific."

"No," said the owner, "the fox terrier is nothing. The Spitz is a ventriloquist."

A man with an interest in show business is walking down a country road and walks by a horse, which says, "Hello, sir, remember me? I won the Kentucky Derby five years back."

A bona fide talking horse, the man thinks as he runs to find its owner.

"That horse is no damn good," says the owner, "but if you really want him, you can have him for twenty dollars."

"Twenty?" the man retorts. "I'll give you two thousand."

"Fine with me, but has that old haybag been giving you that malarkey about winning the Derby? I happen to know it was the Preakness, and he didn't even win."

Two sardines are discussing tennis and one says, "I've got a great idea, let's go to Forest Hills this year."
"How would we get there?" says the second.
"On the Long Island Rail Road," says the first.
"What, and get packed in like commuters?"

"Won't you let me lead one of my own lives?" said the put-upon young cat to its parents.

A worm coming out of the warm spring earth looked around and saw another worm looking at him.
"I love you," he said.
"Don't be silly, I'm your other end."

A man goes to the zoo and carefully positions himself close enough to one of the camels so he can drop a straw squarely on its back.
The camel turns his head. "Wrong straw."

A man in a movie theater notices what looks like a bear sitting next to him.
"Are you a bear?"
"Yes."
"What are you doing at the movies?"
"Well, I liked the book."

"It's cruel," said the papa bear to his family on seeing a carload of humans, "to keep them caged up like that."

"I've finally got him trained," said the first laboratory rat to the second. "Every time I go through the maze and press the bar he gives me a piece of cheese."

"Doc," says the leopard to his neurologist, "every time I look at my wife I see spots."

"That's quite normal."

"But you don't understand. My wife's a tiger."

A dog walks into a telegraph office, takes out a blank form, and writes, "Woof, woof, woof, woof, woof, woof, woof, woof, woof."

The clerk looks at it and says, "There are only nine words here; you could send another woof for the same price."

"But," the dog replies, "that would be silly."

A group of ostriches held regular meetings and were quite annoyed by Ostrich Bill, who was always late. Once they decided to play a trick on him and hide before he arrived. As they saw Bill approach, they all buried their heads in the sand.

Bill arrived, looked around, and said, "Well, well— I finally got here ahead of all of them."

2. Stories Not About Animals

A man staggers off the train obviously suffering from the worst sort of travel sickness.

"What happened?" his wife asks.

"Backwards . . . riding backwards . . . sick . . . makes me sick."

"My poor dear," she says, "but why didn't you ask the party sitting opposite you to change seats?"

"Couldn't," says the sick man. "There wasn't anyone there."

Aereo the Magnificent finally convinces a hard-bitten Hollywood agent to have a look at his act. He drags the agent to Madison Square Garden, which is set up for the circus, which is just coming to town.

The performer takes off his robe, begins flapping his arms, and within moments is airborne. As he gains speed and altitude, he starts a dazzling show of trick aircraft maneuvers, including one in which he starts with a barrel roll, goes into a falling leaf, and regains power after dropping to within a foot of the floor. After twenty minutes of this he lands in front of the agent.

The agent takes a puff on his cigar and says, "So what else do you do besides bird impressions?"

A company found that it could make a new and remarkable line of cosmetics from the skins of bullfrogs. Immediately it began advertising for frog skins, and one of the first replies was a telegram from a farmer in Texas who stated:

CAN SEND ANY QUANTITY UP TO 100,000. ADVISE.

A telegram was sent back asking for the full hundred thousand.

A week later a small box arrived from the farmer with one dried bullfrog skin and a note: "This is all there was. The noise sure had me fooled."

The man was bleeding profusely from the ear when he came into the emergency room screaming, "I bit myself, I bit myself."

"That's impossible," said the intern on duty. "How can a man bit himself on the ear?"

The man replied, "I was standing on a chair."

A magician shows his agent his new act in which he makes two hundred cigars appear out of thin air, takes a puff on each, and then swallows them one at a time until they're all gone.

"That's amazing," says the agent. "How do you manage to do it?"

"Very simple," says the magician. "I get the cigars wholesale from a cousin in Tampa."

A man visits his elderly father, who lives alone in a small apartment above his store.

"Dad, I really worry about you. You work alone all day in the store and then come up here where you're alone. You really should develop some outside interests."

"Son," he replies, "it's not as bad as it looks. You see, I've got a hobby. I keep bees."

"You keep bees in this tiny apartment? Where could you possibly house them?" asks the son.

"There, over there on the table in a glass jar."

"But those bees will suffocate, that jar has a lid on it."

"What do I care?" says the father. "It's only a hobby."

"Number twenty-three," yelled the man from the bar at a nightclub. It was followed by a roar of laughter from around the room.

A newcomer asked one of the old-timers what was going on.

"Well it's like this, we've all been together for years, and we know each other's jokes. A while back we decided to compile a numbered list of our favorites, so that all you have to do is mention the number and everyone can recall the story."

"That's great," said the newcomer. "Let me see the list and try one out."

He looked at the list, spotted the funniest joke, and shouted out, "Number eleven!"

There was a deathly silence, yet he tried again. "Number eleven." The silence continued.

"Why did they laugh at twenty-three and not at eleven?" he asked the old-timer.

"Well, you see," said the older man, "it isn't the joke so much as the way you tell it."

Each day at the end of office hours, a veterinarian stops at a bar for a drink. One day he notices that the owner's cat is getting fat. He examines the cat and tells him, "Pat, this cat is pregnant."

"Impossible," says the owner. "That cat has never been out of my sight."

Each time the vet comes in he repeats the diagnosis and each time the owner insists that the cat never had the opportunity.

One day the vet comes in and a huge tomcat walks out from under the bar.

"There, there," says the vet, "there's the father."

"Don't be silly," says the owner. "That's her cousin."

A traveling salesman knocked on the farmer's door late one night requesting a place to bed down.

"We're a mite tight on space," said the farmer, "so I'm going to have to put you in with my three sons."

"Pardon me," said the salesman, "I must be in the wrong joke."

A man who had gambled away every last cent in Las Vegas was forced to borrow a dime to use the rest-room pay toilet. When he got to the men's room he found an unlocked stall and knew he had one last dime to use in a slot machine. He used the dime, hit the jackpot, and parlayed that jackpot into millions of dollars.

Now rich and famous, he went on a lecture tour telling his story and then declaring that if he ever found his benefactor he would split his fortune with him.

After he'd given his lecture a few thousand times, a man finally jumped up and declared, "I'm him. I'm the man who gave you the dime for the toilet."

"You're not the one," the lucky man shot back. "I'm looking for a guy who left the door open."

The old veteran had been given the job by the city of polishing the cannon in the civic center each day. When it came time for him to retire, they asked him what he was going to do with his leisure time, and he announced that he was going to buy a cannon and go into business for himself.

A newspaper reporter convinces the new circus midget to grant him a Sunday interview. The reporter arrives and a man close to six feet tall answers the door.

"I'm looking for Mr. Tiny."

"That's me."

"What?"

"I told you that this was my day off."

3. Animals at Bars

A man walks into a bar and orders two martinis: one for himself and one for his poodle. This goes on for a number of nights until a night comes in which the poodle comes in alone and says, "I'm sorry, my master isn't feeling well tonight, so perhaps you could give me my martini and he will pay for it tomorrow."

The bartender says fine and serves the dog his drink.

The next night the man and the poodle come in and the man says, "Thank you so much for being so kind to my poodle. In fact I've brought you a gift."

The bartender opens the gift box and finds a large, live lobster.

"Thank you, sir," says the bartender. "I'll take it home to dinner."

"Oh, she's already had her dinner," says the man, "take her to a movie."

A grasshopper hops onto a bar and the bartender turns to him and says, "Hi, little fellow, did you know that we serve a drink here that's named after you?"

The grasshopper looks at him with surprise and says, "You mean to say you have a drink named Irving?"

The bartender is startled as a great white shark slides through the door of his bar.

Sensing something wrong, the shark says, "It's okay Mac, I'm over twenty-one."

A man walks into a bar with a frog growing out of his ear.

"When did you first notice it?" the bartender asks.

"It started as a wart," replies the frog.

A rabbit and a lion come into a bar together and order martinis.

The bartender puts out a bowl of peanuts, a bowl of popcorn, and a bowl of pretzels which the rabbit begins eating. The lion just sips his martini.

"What's the matter?" asks the bartender of the lion. "Aren't you hungry?"

"Don't be silly," the rabbit answers. "If he were hungry, do you think I'd be sitting here?"

A man walks into a Third Avenue bar with his dog and orders two Manhattans: one for himself and one for the dog. Both knock back their drinks, eat the peels and cherries, chew up the glasses, and then spit the stems over their shoulders.

The process is repeated three times. Finally the man takes a look at the bartender, puts his arm around the dog, and says, "I bet you think we're crazy, don't you?"

"I sure do, the stem's the best part."

A gorilla walks into a bar with a banana tucked behind his ear. The bartender, a man of great restraint, decides he will not ask the gorilla about the banana because he figures it was placed there to get a rise out of him. Each day for forty-two days the gorilla comes in with the banana and the bartender never mentions it.

Finally on the forty-third day the gorilla arrives with a carrot behind his ear. The bartender can't stand it any longer.

"Okay, what's the story with the carrot?"

"Couldn't find a banana today," the gorilla explains.

 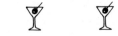

A man comes into a bar with a small white mouse in his pocket. He puts the mouse on the bar and orders a martini for himself and a thimbleful for the mouse.

After downing the drink, the mouse stands on its hind legs and sings a medley of songs from *My Fair Lady*.

The bartender is amazed.

"Listen," says the man, "buy us a round and you can keep the mouse."

The bartender serves the drinks and then says, "I can't believe that you're giving away a gold mine like that for a few drinks."

"Hell," says the mouse's former owner, "all he knows is *My Fair Lady*."

A horse walks into a bar and orders a vodka martini, medium dry, shaken, not stirred.

A customer sits with his mouth open and his eyes

agog while the horse sips the martini and chats with the bartender. After about fifteen minutes the horse gets up and walks out.

"Did you see that?" says the customer.

"See what?" the bartender says.

"That horse," the guys says, "the one that came in here, ordered a vodka martini, and sat around chatting with you for fifteen minutes. Don't you think that is a little unusual?"

"Yeah, now that you mention it," the bartender says, "he used to order gin martinis."

A well-known actor comes into a bar with a gorilla and two martinis are ordered.

The bartender then says to the actor, "Okay, what can he do—sing? tell jokes? dance? act? what?"

"Nothing," replies the actor.

"Then why did you bring him into this joke?" the bartender asks.

"He's my agent," says the actor.

An actor who had a trained dog act and was something of a ventriloquist found himself broke and far from home. Entering a bar, he placed his dog on the stool next to him and ordered a drink. As the bartender made the drink, the dog asked for a martini.

"Who said that?" said the bartender.

"My dog," said the actor. "He can talk."

The bartender was fascinated and while the man and dog had their drinks, he chatted with them. Finally he said to the man, "Your dog fascinates me. I'd like to buy him and I'll offer you one hundred dollars."

"Out of the question," said the man. "I'd want a lot more than that."

The two dickered for a while and the bartender finally agreed to pay the actor $350 in cash.

Just as the actor was getting up to leave, the dog turned his head and said, "Wait a second, do I under-

stand that you are going to sell me to this man for a
mere three hundred fifty dollars?"

"Yes," said the actor, heading for the door.

"Well," said the dog, "just for that, I'll never say another word as long as I live."

A man trained his dog to carry an empty bucket to
the corner saloon and bring it back filled with beer.
He paid for the beer by tucking a dollar into the dog's
collar. Not having a dollar one day, he tucked a five
into the dog's collar.

When the dog did not return, he walked to the saloon
and found the dog seated at the bar drinking a double
martini.

"You never did anything like this before," said the
dog's master.

"I never had the money before," replied the dog.

A lion walks into a bar and orders a dry martini.
"What does a lion know?" thinks the bartender, and
charges the lion ten dollars. After a while the bartender's curiosity gets the best of him: he walks over to
him, starts wiping the bar, casual-like, looks up, and
says, "Say, you know, we don't get too many lions in
here."

Says the lion, "I'm not surprised, at these prices."

A man enters a bar intent on a martini when he notices that the bar is being tended by a horse in an apron.

"'S'matter," says the horse as he drops an olive in
the martini, "ain't ya ever seen a horse before?"

"No! No! It's not what you think," he says. "I'm just
shocked that the cow that used to own this gold mine
sold it."

The Willies

Before there were sick jokes, there were Little Willies: compact, paired couplets filled with deep meanness. In his *Humor of Humor,* Evan Esar traced them back to 1899 and a sadistic little volume, *Ruthless Rhymes for Heartless Homes,* by an English poet named Harry Graham.

Graham's most famous rhyme:

Billy, in one of his nice new sashes,
Fell in the fire and was burned to ashes;
Now, although the room grows chilly
I haven't the heart to poke poor Billy.

Billy gave way to Willie and hundreds of Little Willie quatrains began appearing, and continued to show up in joke magazines right through the 1950s. It is a shame that they have gone out of vogue. It is hard to find one that isn't a gem:

Willie saw some dynamite,
Couldn't understand it quite.
Curiosity never pays;
It rained Willie several days.

Willie, in his roguish way
Pushed Grandpa into the fire one day.
Mother said, "My dear, that's cruel!
But of course it *does* save fuel."

Willie, with an awful curse
Threw a saucepan at his nurse.
When he hit her on the nose,
Mother cried, "How straight he throws."

Willie split the baby's head,
To see if brains were gray or red.
Mother, troubled, said to Father,
"Children are an awful bother!"

Willie's cute as cute can be!
Beneath his brother, only three,
He lit a stick of dynamite.
Now Bubby's simply out of sight!

Into the cistern little Willie
Pushed his little sister Lily.
Mother couldn't find her daughter:
Now we sterilize our water.

Willie, hitting at a ball,
Lined one down the schoolhouse hall
Through his door came Dr. Hill.
Several teeth are missing still.

Willie poisoned his father's tea;
Father died in agony.
Mother came, and looked quite vexed:
"Really, Will," she said, "what next?"

Little Willie hung his sister;
She was dead before we missed her.
"Willie's always up to tricks.
Ain't he cute? He's only six!"

Little Will, with Father's gun,
Punctured Grandma, just for fun.
Mother frowned at the merry lad:
It was the last shell Father had.

Willie took a pair of shears,
Cut off both the baby's ears;
At the baby, so unsightly,
Mama raised her eyebrows slightly.

Willie, looking down the gun,
Pulls the trigger "just for fun."
Mother says in accents pained—
"Willie is so scatterbrained."

Baby's in the ice-cream freezer.
Willie turns the crank to squeeze her;
Ma says: "Dear, the way that's fixed
You'll have that child completely mixed."

Willie, while the ice was thin,
Tried to skate and he fell in.
Willie tasted rather nice,
When they cut the pond for ice.

Willie stopped a cable car
While standing on the track.
It gave his system quite a jar—
His sisters now wear black.

Willie pushed his Aunt Elizer
Off a rock into a geyser;
Now he's feeling quite dejected—
Didn't get the rise expected.

Little Willie wrote a book,
Woman was the theme he took,
Woman was the only text.
Ain't he cute? He's oversexed.

Little Willie killed his sister,
A thing a brother should not do;
Cried his mother: "Now you'll catch it,
You've spoiled your father's brand-new hatchet!"

Little Willie, with a rock,
Beaned the cuckoo in the clock.
Father said: "Why don't it tick?"
Willie said: "The bird is sick."

He shot at Lee Wing,
But he winged Willie Wong;
A slight but regrettable
Slip of the tong.

Our Willie studied chemistry,
But Willie is no more.
What he took for H_2O
Was H_2SO_4.

Little Willie;
Pair of skates;
Hole in the ice;
Golden gates.

Willie in the cauldron fell;
See the grief on Mother's brow!
Mother loved her darling well;
Darling's quite hard-boiled by now.

Little Willie from the mirror licked the mercury
right off,
Thinking, in his childish error, it would cure
his whooping cough.
At the funeral Willie's mother sadly said to Mrs.
Brown,
"'Twas a chilly day for Willie when the mercury
went down!"

Willie fell down the elevator—
Wasn't found till six days later.
Then the neighbors sniffed. "Gee whiz!
What a spoiled child Willie is!"

Willie on the railroad track—
The engine gave a squeal.
The engineer just took a spade
And scraped him off the wheel.

Willie, with a thirst for gore,
Nailed the baby to the door.
Mother said, with humor quaint,
"Willie, dear, don't spoil the paint."

While most of these rhymes featured Willie himself,
it was permissible to bring other gruesome characters
into the act.

Father nailed his darling wife
Fast against the parquet flooring.
Tho' he was loath to take her life,
He simply had to stop her snoring.

We'll never bail our brat,
No more we'll pay his fines.
He hung himself with Dad's cravat—
Blest be the tie that binds.

My darling wife was always glum.
I drowned her in a cask of rum,
And so made sure that she would stay
In better spirits night and day.

Lucy met a train
The train met Lucy
The track was juicy
The juice was Lucy.

Father, I regret to state,
Cut his daughters up for bait.

We miss them when it's time to dine.
But Father's fish taste simply fine.

Oh, tell me, Mother, what is that?
It looks like strawberry jam.
Hush, hush, my child, it's only Pa
Run over by a tram.

Merry funny little Moses
Burnt off both his brothers' noses;
And it made them look so queer
Mama said: "Why, Moses dear!"

Sam had spirits naught could check,
And today, at breakfast, he
Broke his baby sister's neck,
So he shan't have jam for tea!

An angel bore dear Uncle Joe
To rest beyond the stars.
I miss him, oh! I miss him so—
He had such good cigars.

Making toast at the fireside
Nurse fell in the fire and died;
And, what makes it ten times worse,
All the toast was burned with Nurse.

Unlike the limerick, which was the first cousin to the Little Willie (the bawdy cousin of the cruel cousin), the Little Willie has not been brought up to date. This is a shame, since there is so much to work with. A few examples begged to be written in hopes of helping to spark a revival.

Willie stole a van from Sears,
Drove it through a field of peers.

Now he said with quite a shout:
My day-care center's all wiped out.

Willie slugged his sitter,
Broke her nose, and bit her.
Why he did is plain to see—
Too much violence on TV.

Making Mary

It is axiomatic that the sweeter and the more innocent the nursery rhyme, the greater is the urge to rewrite it with the same venomous pen that gave us the vile Willie.

Here is some of what several generations of anonymous doggerelists have done to Mary, her lamb, and her contrariness.

Mary had a little watch
She swallowed it one day.
Now she's taking Epsom salts
To pass the time away.

Mary had a kitten,
Tommy had a pup,
Alphonse had a crocodile,
Which ate the others up.

Mary had a little calf,
She showed it very well;
There were women on the jury.
Now Mary is in a cell.

Mary had a little lamb,
Also a little bear.
I've often seen her little lamb—
My story ends right there.

Mary had a little lime
And quite a lot of gin,
And everywhere that Mary went
She didn't know she'd been.

Mary had a little lamb,
The lamb had halitosis,
And everywhere that Mary went
The people held their nosis.

Mary had a little pet—
'Twas neither lamb nor gopher.
She most enjoyed her little pet
Upon the parlor sofa.

Mary had a little lamb,
But the boys gave her no tumble.
Now Mary's grown and has two calves
That make the boys all mumble.

Mary had a bathing suit,
The latest style, no doubt;
And when she got inside it she
Was more than halfway out.

Little Mary on the ice
Went with her friends to frisk
Wasn't Mary being nice,
Her pretty * ?

Mary had a little lamb
Before she learned to think
Now she's blond and men are fond
Of keeping her in mink.

Mary had a little swing,
It isn't hard to find,
And everywhere that Mary goes
The swing is just behind!

Mary had a little lamb,
A lobster and some prunes,
A glass of milk, a piece of pie,
And then some macaroons.
It made the naughty waiters grin
To see her order so,
And when they carried Mary out
Her face was white as snow.

Mary had a little lamb,
Its feet were black as soot
And everywhere that Mary went
His sooty foot he put.

Mistress Mary, quite contrary,
Just lets her mustache grow—
"Why should I take such pains," she says,
"To please the average Joe?"

Mary, Mary quite contrary,
What does your garden grow?
"Silver bells and cockleshells
And one damn petunia."

Punishments

No collection of puns would be complete without a collection of these:

Acoustic: Instrument used in billiards.
Alarms: Describing an octopus.
Aseptic: Doubter with a cold.
Aspire: How Cleopatra died.
Asterisk: Hazard in space.
Austere: Source of *au jus.*
Autopsy: Roof of a car.
Aversion: One side of a disputed story.

Bacteria: The rear portion of a cafeteria.
Bandeau: Forbidden French water.
Bar Stool: What Davy Crockett stepped in.
Beckon: Meat from the sides of a hog.
Bigamist: Fog in Italy.
Bigamy: Large pigmy.
Bullion: Mythical beast, half bull, half lion.
Buoyant: Male insect.

Camelot: Where humped beasts are parked.
Candle: Jarred pickles?
Cantilever: State of male monogamy.
Category: Cat run over by steamroller, also long puss.
Cello: German Jell-O.
Cherub: Furniture polish.
Cistern: Opposite of brethren.
Cochineal: To bash a small, narrow fish.
Coincide: What you do when it starts to rain.

Collapse: How an audience reacts to a performance.
Comatose: Foot grooming.
Commentator: Undistinguished potato.
Conceit: Eye strain.
Condense: Prison prom.
Condominium: Midget's birth control device.
Coward: Bovine direction.
Crocodile: Jar of soap.
Cruelty: Difficult hole in golf.
Custody: Custardlike.

Debate: What lures de fish.
Decontrol: Ugly church officer who lives in a cave.
Denial: Egyptian river.
Despair: Tire kept for emergencies.
Dictum: Harry's two companions.
Digest: Morbid joke.
Diploma: The person who fixes the pipes.
Documentate: What you say to the doctor when he charges you ten dollars for an eight-dollar procedure.
Domineer: Cheap corn, as contrasted with buccaneer, expensive corn.
Dromedary: Store that sells milk to camels.
Dulcet: Inferior tennis.

Eclipse: What the gardener does to the hedge.
Elliptical: A kiss.
Exorbitant: A costly satellite which has fallen out of the sky.

Farcical: Long bike ride.
Fulgent: Man after a large dinner.
Fungi: A comedian; the life of the party.
Furlong: The hair on a shaggy dog.

Geometry: What an acorn says when it is grown up.
Gneiss: Compliment made to metamorphic rocks.
Grimace: Ace of spades.

Hypotenuse: Washroom upstairs is occupied.

Hypothesis: Opening words when a child calls home.

Igloo: Eskimo toilet.
Impunity: Agreement among devils.
Incongruous: Where our laws are made.
Innuendo: Italian for Preparation H.
Isolate: Rabbit's exclamation from *Alice in Wonderland.*

Japonica: Imported vehicle.

Kennel: Waterway.
Kimono: Japanese refusal to mow lawn.

Laundress: Garb for outdoor party.
Lithe: Told by bad boys.
Locus: Obscene muttering.
Logarithm: Song sung in the north woods.
Lubber: Rubber in Japan.
Lugubrious: Fond of peanuts.

Macadam: The first Scotsman.
Marigold: Find a rich spouse.
Meretricious: Seasonal greeting, with "Happy New Year."
Metronome: Subway pixie.
Mycologist: Loyal alumnus.

Obituary: Snake's exclamation after biting man.
Oboe: British bum.
Ohm: Englishman's castle.
Oscilloscope: Meter that often gives ridiculous readings.

Paradox: Medical partnership.
Pasteurize: Too far to see.
Paucity: Depressed municipality.
Politics: A parrot that has swallowed a watch.
Polygon: Dead parrot.
Preternatural: Additive-free preter.
Program: Metric advocate.

Ptarmigan: Pbird.

Quadrillion: Dance requiring four million participants.
Quoit: Absolutely.

Rheumatic: Upper apartment.

Specimen: Italian astronaut.
Staple: Irish church tower.
Stoic: Bird which brings babies.
Suburban: Liquor served on a submarine.

Tangent: Man returned from the beach.
Tirade: Retaliation for panty raid.
Torque: Tortured conversation.
Toupee: Dutch treat.

Uranium: Storm exclamation.

Valorus: Large animal vit tusks; lives in vater.
Variola: Ancient.
Velocity: We lost a hot drink.
Violin: Bad hotel.

Warehouse: Cry of person lost in blizzard.
Wino: Opposite of "Why, yes."

Xerophyte: No argument.

Zealotry: What a tree salesman likes to do.

Many Hands Make Light Work

They took off in the late 1970s, continue to multiply, and are as clear an example as can be found that formula jokes are still an extremely hot item. Their lineage is clear. The first was an older Aggie/Polish/Finn slur joke:

Q. How many ——————— does it take to screw in a light bulb?
    A. Five. One to hold the bulb and four to turn the chair.

Suddenly you heard them everywhere and before long they were being discussed in academic journals in terms of profound social trends— ". . . we are joking about our own potential lack of sexual and political power," said Alan Dundes in *Western Folklore,* and Judith B. Kerman used the pages of the *Journal of American Folklore* to term them a metaphor for "social action and decision making in technological times. . . ."

On a more overt level they were throwbacks, an excuse for stereotyping in an age when stereotyping wasn't acceptable.

Here is one of the largest collections in captivity carefully assembled to insult just about everybody.

Q. How many *Americans* . . .
    A. One.

Q. How many *auto mechanics* . . .

A. Six. One to force it with a hammer and five to go out for more bulbs.

Q. How many *ayatollahs* . . .
A. None. There were no light bulbs in the thirteenth century.

Q. How many *baby-sitters* . . .
A. None. They don't make Pampers small enough.

Q. How many *bankers* . . .
A. Four. One to hold the bulb and three to try to remember the combination.

Q. How many *Beverly Hills realtors* . . .
A. Three. One to screw it in and two to learn Farsi.

Q. How many *bluegrass musicians* . . .
A. One to screw it in and one to complain that it's electrified.

Q. How many *British Navy officers* . . .
A. Only one, but it takes him seven weeks to get there.
    (This was popular during the Falklands crisis.)

Q. How many *bureaucrats* . . .
A. One to spot the burned-out bulb, his supervisor to authorize a requisition, a requisition typist, twelve clerks to file requisition copies, a mail clerk to deliver the requisition to the purchasing department, a purchasing agent to order the bulb, a clerk to forward the purchasing order, a clerk to mail-order, a receiving clerk to receive the bulb . . .

A. One to screw it in, one to screw it up.
A. None. "We contract out for things like that."
A. One, but he'll need two outside consultants to help.
A. Two. One to assure us that everything possible is being done while the other screws the bulb into a water faucet.

Q. How many *Californians* . . .
A. Three. One to change the bulb and two to share the experience.
A. Three. One to change the bulb and two to say, "Oh, wow!"
A. None. Californians don't screw in light bulbs, they screw in hot tubs.

Q. How many *Californians* does it take to water a plant?
A. Two. One to pour the Perrier and one to massage the leaves.

Q. How many *college basketball players* . . .
A. Only one, but he gets three credits for doing it.

Q. How many *computerists* . . .
A. None. Real computerists only use LEDs.
(This is one of twelve answers to this question developed by Jim Rubins of Napa, California. Most could only be truly appreciated by computerists; e.g., "Hundreds have died trying to put a ± 5-volt device in a 110-volt peripheral slot," or "That depends on how unreadable the documentation is.")

Q. How many *doctors* . . .
A. That depends on whether or not it has health insurance.

Q. How many *editors* . . .
A. Two, one to change the bulb and one to issue a rejection slip to the old bulb.

Q. How many *European ballet troupes* . . .
A. None. They like Danzig in the dark.

Q. How many *evolutionists* . . .
A. Only one, but it takes him eight million years.

Q. How many *feminists* . . .
A. "Hey! Watch it, buster!"

A. "That isn't funny."

A. Two. One to change the bulb, and one to write about how it feels.

A. Five. One to change the bulb, two to discuss the violation of the socket, and two to secretly wish that they were that socket.

Q. How many *firemen* . . .
A. Four. One to change the bulb and three to cut a hole in the roof.

Q. How many *gay men* . . .
A. Five. One to screw it in and four to stand back and say, "It's to die."

Q. How many *graduate students* . . .
A. Only one, but it takes him seven years.
A. Two, and a professor to take credit.
A. It all depends on the size of the grant.

Q. How many *grocery store cashiers* . . .
A. Are you kidding? They won't even change a five-dollar bill.

Q. How many *humor theorists* . . .
A. Three hundred. One to change the bulb and two hundred ninety-nine to analyze it to death.

(This appeared in *The Washington Post* of August 30, 1982, where it was attributed to Desmond McHale of Cork, Ireland, at the end of the Third International Conference on Humor. McHale was reacting to such topics as "The Early Development of Children's Appreciation of Disparagement Humor" and "Humor in Contemporary American and European Architecture.")

Q. How many *Iranians* . . .
A. One hundred. One to screw it in and ninety-nine to hold the house hostage.

Q. How many *Japanese industrialists* . . .
A. Three. One to make sure the new bulb is not foreign, one to change the bulb, and one to look into the export potential of the old bulb.

Q. How many *Jewish American princesses* . . .
A. Four. One to call Daddy and three to run out for Diet Pepsis.
A. One who refuses, saying, "What, and ruin my nail polish?"

Q. How many *Jewish mothers* . . .
A. None. "It's all right, I'll just sit here in the dark."

Q. How many *jerks who ask stupid questions* . . .
A. Change it to what?

Q. How many *Kentuckians* (Nebraskans, etc.) . . .
A. What's a light bulb?

Q. How many *liberals* . . .
A. One liberal and twenty-eight delegates representing all the social, economic, and ethnic communities.

Q. How many *loggers* . . .
A. One, but he uses a chain saw.

Q. How many *Marinites* . . .
A. Five. One to screw it in and four to sit in the hot tub and discuss the environmental impact.

Q. How many *Martians* does it take to screw *in* a light bulb?
A. Two, but they're very tiny.

Q. How many *massage parlor attendants* . . .
A. Whatever number turns you on, big boy.

Q. How many *medflies* . . .
A. None. They do it in the fruit.

Q. How many *New Yorkers* . . .
A. "None of your damn business."

A. Five. One to change the bulb and four to protect him from muggers.

A. Two hundred and one. One to put it in and two hundred to watch it happen without trying to stop it.

Q. How many *newsmen* ...
A. Only one, but he'll tell everybody.

Q. How many *Pennsylvanians* ...
A. None. You just hold it up and it glows by itself. (Three Mile Island. Get it?)

Q. How many *pessimists* ...
A. None. The old one is probably screwed in too tight.

Q. How many *poets* ...
A. Three. One to curse the darkness, one to light a candle, and one to change the bulb.

Q. How many *police officers* ...
A. Just one, but he's never around when you need him.

Q. How many *premeds* ...
A. Three. One to stand on the stool and screw it in and two to kick the stool out from under him.

Q. How many *procrastinators* ...
A. Only one, but he's got to wait until the light is better.

Q. How many *psychiatrists* ...
A. Only one—but the light bulb has to really *want* to change.
A. Only one—but it will take a very long time and will be very expensive.

Q. How many *real men* ...
A. None. Real men aren't afraid of the dark.

Q. How many *right-wing economists* ...
A. None. They let the market do it.

Q. How many *Russians* . . .
A. That is a military secret.

Q. How many *sex therapists* . . .
A. Two. One to screw it in, and one to tell him he's screwing it in the wrong way.

Q. How many *straight San Franciscans* . . .
A. Both of them.

Q. How many *software engineers* . . .
A. None. It's a hardware problem.

Q. How many *Tampa Bay Buccaneers* (Baltimore Colts, etc.) . . .
A. Two. One to screw it in and the other to re-cover the fumble.

Q. How many *teachers* . . .
A. One if at home, but on school time, four.

Q. How many *terrorists* . . .
A. Twenty. One to do it, nineteen to develop a distraction.

Q. How many *Virginians* . . .
A. Three. One to change it and two to sit around reminiscing about how good the old bulb was.

Q. How many *waiters* . . .
A. None. Even a burned-out bulb can't catch a waiter's eye.

Q. How many *WASPs* . . .
A. Two. One to call the electrician and one to mix the martinis.

Q. How many *White House aides* . . .
A. They prefer to do it in the dark.

Q. How many *Zen Buddhists* . . .
A. Two. One to screw it in and one not to screw it in.

Q. How many *Zen masters* . . .
  A. The Zen master is the light bulb.

Fort Knocks —
The Master Collector

Believe it or not, the English-speaking world harbors more than a few serious knock-knock joke collectors. Charles Orr, a retired gentleman living in Healdsburg, California, claims to have the largest collection. He now has more than 131,000 of them and is creating and collecting new ones daily. Orr, who hopes to have his collection recognized by the *Guinness Book* as a world's record, is a generous man who has permitted me to use some of his recent state-of-the-art additions here.

Knock, Knock.
Who's there?
Adage.
Adage who?
Adage where all I can do is look!

Knock, Knock.
Who's there?
Adam.
Adam who?
Adam fly is in my soup.

Knock, Knock.
Who's there?
Al Bedouin.
Al Bedouin who?
Al Bedouin-ter like this one will be long remembered.

Knock, Knock
Who's there?
Alicia.
Alicia who?
Alicia like me a little bit, don't you?

Knock, Knock.
Who's there?
Anita Loos.
Anita Loos who?
Anita Loos about twenty pounds.

Knock, Knock.
Who's there?
Anwar.
Anwar who?
Anwar sorry about the rain delay!

Knock, Knock.
Who's there?
Asimov.
Asimov who?
Asimov-ie it's even better.

Knock, Knock.
Who's there?
Avery and Happy.
Avery and Happy who?
Avery meretricious and a Happy New Year!

Knock, Knock.
Who's there?
Cat gut.
Cat gut who?
Cat gut your tongue?

Knock, Knock.
Who's there?

Chiquita.
Chiquita who?
Chiquita little last night?

Knock, Knock.
Who's there?
Censure.
Censure who?
Censure so smart, why aren't you rich?

Knock, Knock.
Who's there?
Codicil.
Codicil who?
I've codicil-y wife.

Knock, Knock.
Who's there?
Creature.
Creature who?
Creature old friend with a hug.

Knock, Knock.
Who's there?
Darwin.
Darwin who?
Darwin young man on the flying trapeze.

Knock, Knock.
Who's there?
Despair.
Despair who?
Despair tire is flat.

Knock, Knock.
Who's there?
Effervescent.
Effervescent who?

Effervescent for wine, women, and song, he'd be
a perfect husband.

Knock, Knock.
Who's there?
Elsewhere.
Elsewhere who?
Elsewhere it's true!

Knock Knock.
Who's there?
Evita.
Evita who?
Evita shut up we wouldn't have gotten a ticket!

Knock, Knock.
Who's there?
Ghana.
Ghana who?
Ghana wash that man right out of my hair.

Knock, Knock.
Who's there?
Gil.
Gil who?
Gil the umpire!

Knock, Knock.
Who's there?
Hair comb.
Hair comb who?
Hair comb the bride!

Knock, Knock.
Who's there?

Hero.
Hero who?
Hero today, gone to Maui!

Knock, Knock.
Who's there?
Hindu.
Hindu who?
Hindu each life a little rain must fall!

Knock, Knock.
Who's there?
Hopi.
Hopi who?
Hopi quiet!

Knock, Knock.
Who's there?
Huron.
Huron who?
Huron my foot.

Knock, Knock.
Who's there?
Hussein.
Hussein who?
Hussein at a time like this?

Knock, Knock.
Who's there?
Ike, Ann, Howard, Lee, Waite, Tillie, Damien,
Sarah, Jane, Jed, and Mary.
Ike, Ann, Howard, Lee, Waite, Tillie, Damien,
Sarah, Jane, Jed, and Mary who?
Ike, Ann, Howard, Lee, Waite, Tillie, Damien,
Sarah, Jane, Jed, and Mary-ed.

Knock, Knock.
Who's there?
Inouye.
Inouye who?
Inouye you want it, big boy!

Knock, Knock.
Who's there?
Ivan.
Ivan who?
Ivan to be alone!

Knock, Knock.
Who's there?
Juanda.
Juanda who?
Juanda make something out of it?

Knock, Knock.
Who's there?
Juarez.
Juarez who?
Juarez hell!

Knock, Knock.
Who's there?
Lecher.
Lecher who?
Lecher hair hang down.

Knock, Knock.
Who's there?
Lilac.
Lilac who?
She can lilac a trooper.

Knock, Knock.
Who's there?

Lipset.
Lipset who?
Lipset taste wine will never taste mine!

Knock, Knock.
Who's there?
Ma Bell.
Ma Bell who?
Ma Bell is out of order—knock!

Knock, Knock.
Who's there?
Macho.
Macho who?
Macho do about nothing.

Knock, Knock.
Who's there?
Mama san.
Mama san who?
Mama san the warpath!

Knock, Knock.
Who's there?
Manor.
Manor who?
Are you a manor a mouse?

Knock, Knock.
Who's there?
Marcus Welby.
Marcus Welby who?
I Marcus Welby dead for all you care!

Knock, Knock.
Who's there?
Nadia.
Nadia who?
Nadia believe me?

Knock, Knock.
Who's there?
Ng.
Ng who?
It's just one little Ng after another.

Knock, Knock.
Who's there?
Nutritious.
Nutritious who?
Nutritious dad would drown in Watergate.

Knock, Knock.
Who's there?
O. A.
O. A. who?
O. A. down south in Dixie!

Knock, Knock.
Who's there?
Omelette.
Omelette who?
Omelette smarter than I look!

Knock, Knock.
Who's there?
Ooze.
Ooze who?
Ooze that knocking at my door?

Knock, Knock.
Who's there?
Opal Lee.
Opal Lee who?
Opal Lees—just for me?

Knock, Knock.
Who's there?
Osmosis.
Osmosis who?
Osmosis, who are you?

Knock, Knock.
Who's there?
Ottawa.
Ottawa who?
Ottawa know St. Peter will let me in?

Knock, Knock.
Who's there?
P.
P. who?
P. U.
(Orr claims this is the shortest ever made.)

Knock, Knock.
Who's there?
Raleigh.
Raleigh who?
Raleigh 'round the flag, boys.

Knock, Knock.
Who's there?
Robin.
Robin who?
Robin Peter to pay Paul!

Knock, Knock.
Who's there?
Rudolph.
Rudolph who?
Money is Rudolph all evil.

Knock, Knock.
Who's there?
Sadie and Eloise.
Sadie and Eloise who?
Sadie word and I'll Eloise be your valentine.

Knock, Knock.
Who's there?
Simi.
Simi who?
Come up and Simi sometime.

Knock, Knock.
Who's there?
Synanon.
Synanon who?
Synanon my salary isn't easy.

Knock, Knock.
Who's there?
Taipei.
Taipei who?
My blood is Taipei.

Knock, Knock.
Who's there?
Wayne.
Wayne who?
Wayne drops keep falling on my head.

Knock, Knock.
Who's there?
Zeus.
Zeus who?
Zeus company, three's a crowd.

The Voice from the Audience

When this project was started, true scientific procedure was followed: formulas were stated, procedures outlined, and objectives listed. But a glaring omission was spotted by Timothy Perper, Ph.D., of Philadelphia. He saw that a key formula was being omitted. Quoting directly from Dr. Perper's communication:

> My favorite genre of formula jokes . . . The Voice from the Balcony/Audience.
>
> A recent and banal example is of the man working on the church ceiling, hidden amidst the rafters. Woman comes, starts to pray, loud and clear, and the painter decides to play a joke, and says thunderingly, *"I have heard your prayer!"* The woman turns, looks up, and says, "Not you, I want to talk to your mother!"
>
> The reason I think that is not funny is that one does not, in this formula joke, ever answer the Voice from the Balcony. It is the voice of the anonymous, faceless crowd, not taken in by nonsense, pretense, and such like. Here is a classic.
>
> Seniors all assembled for their graduation from Barnard College, with their parents, etc., etc., all dressed up, etc., etc. The Dean, an older woman, is going on and on. "Body and mind both healthy [etc.], responsibility of womanhood [etc.], love is basic to family [etc.], not cast away promiscuously [etc.], young lady's responsibility to eschew

promiscuous sex [rave, rant], dangers of wantonness [rr], pleasures of sex only transient [rr], unwanted pregnancy [rr], VD [rr, but euphemistically], loss of respectability, loss of femininity, loss of grace, rave, rant . . . and for what? All cast away for naught but *an hour of pleasure!*"

Voice from audience: "How do you make it last an hour?"

And, perhaps, you have not heard (or not heard often) . . .

This was told to me as a classic of the early days of sex education, presumably just after Kinsey, when delicately and with trouble, U.S. colleges and universities were grudgingly first introducing the rudiments of sex education. And, of course, like all such stories, it was sworn to be true.

The instructor (male) was explaining something of the anatomy of the sexual organs. He had reached a description of the male genitalia, and was—with difficulty—trying to conquer his embarrassment in describing the testicles. "The human male's testicles," he said, "are approximately the size and shape of plover's eggs. . . ." [In fact, early sex education texts said precisely that, so that part is true.]

Voice from audience (female): "Well, now we know how large plover's eggs are."

Indeed, these are classics and Perper's work is important. Here are some other examples of the genre:

A new tenor makes his debut at the Met. He sings an aria and the applause is so overwhelming that he sings it again. They try to go on with the opera but the applause won't stop, so he is brought forward to sing it again. This goes on until he has sung it eight times.

Finally he steps forward and addresses his audience: "My friends, this is too much. The honor you have bestowed on me is overwhelming and no matter what becomes of me in the future, this will have been my greatest operatic moment. However, the opera must go on and my voice is tiring, so please don't ask me to sing it again."

Voice from the balcony: "You'll sing it till you get it right!"

Preacher: "... and furthermore, hell is filled with cocktails, roulette wheels, and naughty chorus girls."

Voice from the rear: "O death, where is thy sting?"

Reformer: "What I want is reform—tax reform, police reform, I want temperance reform, I want social reform, I want—I want—"

Voice from the rear: "What you want is chloroform."

A professor, suspecting that his class was not paying attention, decided to lapse into doubletalk in the midst of his lecture to see if his students were awake:

"The other problems associated with durnamic smolg is resorial, remtious, and refrominating policies of pullic garbistan. As is now becoming clearer, wallage, brough tabs and, occasionally, blinger twetchel are the only possible remedies."

Voice from the rear: "Fine, but what the hell are brough tabs?"

A man comes home unexpectedly one afternoon to find his wife in a negligee and the smell of cigar smoke hanging heavy in the air.

"Where," he demanded, "did the cigar come from?"

Voice from the closet: "Tampa."

The students were slow in bringing in their four dollars for the high-school yearbook and the teacher decided to put some pressure on her class.

"Just think," she said, "twenty-five years from now you can look in this book and say, 'There's Judy Jones, she's an important lawyer today, and here's Tom Smith, who's a doctor, and here's—' "

Voice from the rear: "And here's the teacher, she's dead."

Graduation speaker: "Remember, you must have initiative and go forward in life. Remember, on every door there is a little sign that says PUSH."

Voice from the rear: "And on the other side it says PULL."

Speaker: "A horrible thing has happened. I've just lost my wallet with five hundred dollars in it. I'll give fifty dollars to anyone who will return it."

Voice in the rear: "I'll give one hundred dollars."

Professor: "Order! Order!"
Voice from the rear: "Beer!"

When Jack Benny was eighty-two years old he appeared in a concert and at one point noted, "I have a violin that was made in 1729."

Voice from the rear: "Did you buy it new?"

Professor: "I will not begin today's lecture until the room settles down."

Voice from the rear: "Go home and sleep it off."

Professor: "If I saw a man beating a donkey and stopped him from doing so, what virtue would I be showing?"

Voice from the rear: "Brotherly love."

Orator at the funeral of a noted gambler: "Ace Muldoon is not dead—he only sleeps."

Voice from the rear: "Hundred dollars says he's dead."

Muldoon's mortality suggests the voice which is heard at the last edge of life:

The children are arguing as to the number of limousines which should be in their father's funeral. The noise gets louder and the arguments more acrimonious.

Voice from the edge: "Help me up and I'll walk."

"Where should the old man be buried?" said one of the children. The question touched off a long discussion on the relative merits of a half-dozen cemeteries.

Voice from the edge: "Surprise me!"

All of this naturally brings up the issue of hecklers—voices from the audience gone out of control. There have been hundreds of great one-liners used to neutralize those voices which can't be stilled with a mere request to be quiet. Here are some of the better examples used over the years by platform speakers and performers:

Sir, if they ever put a price on your head, take it.

This man's not himself today—and it's a great improvement.

You're snappy on the comeback—just like your checks.

Please don't talk while I'm interrupting.

There, ladies and gentlemen, is the greatest argument yet advanced for twin beds.

Lady, you wouldn't like it if I came to the place where you worked and turned out the red light.

Sir, you have more nerve than an abscessed tooth.

When I was a kid on the farm I accidentally killed our donkey with an ax and my father told me that someday that jackass would come back to haunt me.

Sir, if Moses had seen you, there would have been another commandment.

Would you mind sitting down, sir, the funny suit contest isn't until later.

Look! The face on the barroom floor just got up.

He loves nature in spite of what it did to him.

That man's always got a chip on his shoulder—his head.

Would you take something downstairs for me?—the elevator.

Tourist Tips

With every newspaper and radio station now giving us all sorts of well-meaning, unsolicited advice on everything from the prevention of poinsettia fungus to wok care, there is something devilishly appealing about intentionally bad advice.

My favorite form is misleading tips for tourists. The tradition was started by the British magazine *New Statesman,* which began asking for wrongheaded tourist advice as London began filling with visitors after World War II. "Visitors in London hotels," wrote one reader, "are expected by the management to hang the bed-linen out of the windows to air." Another suggested, "If you take a taxi, the driver will be only too willing to give your shoes a polish while waiting at the traffic lights."

Inspired by the London example, I developed a list for Washington, D.C.

1. Good-natured heckling from the visitors' gallery of the Senate is a custom as old as the Republic.

2. Try the magnificent echo in the main reading room of the Library of Congress.

3. Wednesday is picture day at the Supreme Court. Pose with the robed judges. Bring the kids.

4. Washington's reputation as "The City of Singing Bus Drivers" is well deserved. Ask and you shall hear.

5. First-time riders on the new Metro subway system are, of course, expected to shake hands with all the passengers in their car on boarding.

6. A little-known 1977 reform act provides that all American citizens have access to the previously private rooms and special services of Congress.

7. One of the Treasury secretary's greatest pleasures comes from personally redeeming matured Savings Bonds. Appointment suggested but not required.

8. Prostitution is under firm control in the District of Columbia. Most work only in daylight and can be found in and around Federal buildings. They can be identified by the plastic ID cards hanging from their necks.

9. Washington's status as an international city is reflected in many ways, including the playful Oriental bazaar at our better stores. In other words, haggling is the order of the day, and if you pay the asking price for an item you will immediately be marked as a rube.

10. Save an afternoon for the Interstate Commerce Commission even if you must pass up the vastly overrated and crowded White House and FBI tours.

11. Call us old fashioned, but our career women still like to be called "girls" even if the gal in question is a member of the Cabinet.

12. Most embassies expect party crashers. ("How else can we get to know 'the people'?" reasons an ambassador from a European nation.)

13. The locals have a great sense of humor and never seem to tire of Carter peanut gags, "Ronnie" jokes, and barbs about red tape and bureaucrats. That old one-liner about Washington being a town of northern charm and southern efficiency still brings down the house.

14. An archaic—but vigorously enforced—law still on the books from the time of the Civil War requires

bar patrons to rise after each drink and assert their sobriety and allegiance to the Union.

15. You can still "do" Washington on fifteen dollars a day, but only if you confine your eating to restaurants with French-sounding names.

After this list of tourist tips appeared in *The Washingtonian* magazine, several others were inspired to create their own, including William D. Tammeus of the *Kansas City Star*, who came up with some useful ideas for his area, among them:

1. Everyone in Kansas City loves and knows all the words to "Everything's Up to Date in Kansas City." Local residents consider it a breach of etiquette if you don't ask them to sing it while you're here.

2. Almost nothing is more fun than going to the stockyards and chatting with the cowboys. They're especially friendly to folks who bring along a little Red Man to chew and share.

3. Visitors who stop by Hallmark Cards are given enough greeting cards to send back home.

4. Small English towns are famous for inexpensive "bed and board" homes for travelers. Bed and board at quite reasonable rates are also available in the Kansas City area. Homes that participate are located exclusively along Ward Parkway, from the Plaza south to Gregory, and in Mission Hills. Just knock on the doors.

5. Sundays are slow news days, so the last ten or twenty minutes of local TV newscasts are reserved for tourists and conventioneers who want to drop by the studios and say "Hi!" to people out there in television land.

6. The custom of bringing your own instruments and

joining in performances of the Kansas City Philhar-
monic is an old one. The more kazoos and tubas, the
better.

7. All major hotels here expect you merely to drop
off the key at the desk when you check out. They'll
bill you later. "It's our way of saying 'Howdy, friend,'"
says one manager.

8. Postcards featuring scenic views of Kansas City,
found in nearly any drugstore, are free. Don't even
bother to ask.

The possibilities are endless—"Never say Dallas
when you're here, it's the Big D" (it's Frisco, too, never
San Francisco); "The guards at Grant's Tomb never
seem to tire of being asked who is buried there"; "You
haven't been to Chicago unless you've complained
about the wind"; "There probably isn't a Canadian
alive who doesn't love being kidded about the influence of the U.S. north of the border"; and "Swedes
just love being told that theirs is just one big moody,
angst-ridden Bergmanesque nation."

It can only be hoped that this inspires more good
advice, which, of course, should be written down, cop-
ied, and placed in guest bedrooms and hotel rooms.

Another fertile field for advice is energy saving. Don
Addis, who illustrated this book, has come up with
these fine bits of advice: ". . . put a cork in unused light
sockets, use less alacrity, let your alarm clock coast,
put a brick in your air conditioner, unplug the electoral
college, turn off your spouse when not in use, set your
microwave on 'stun,' set your blender on 'off' and your
can opener at thirty-three and a third, organize a block
blackout, push your riding mower, and join a moped
pool. To show your support, turn off all your lights all
night."

Slurred Visions

For those who hold to the premise that the best offense is a good offensive joke, here are the four major categories, collected and sorted for handy aggression.

1. Mibbies

Slurring is a popular and long-established avocation among college students and grads. In Texas they are told about Texas A&M and are called Aggie jokes.* They tell them about Georgia Tech at Georgia and about Georgia at Georgia Tech and so forth. The best are Mibbie Jokes, which are told about the dumb-as-a-post students and alumni of Marble State.

The Mibbie football team—nicknamed the Blockheads—no longer gets ice water. The player with the recipe graduated.

Then there was the Mibbie who lost forty dollars on a televised college football game. He dropped twenty dollars on the game and another twenty dollars on the replay.

---

*At Texas A&M they tell Teasip jokes; the name refers to University of Texas students. A current example: An Aggie grad is forced to rent an outhouse because nobody will rent an Aggie an apartment in Austin. His mother comes to visit him and says, "How can you live like this?" The grad answers, "There are worse places to live than this. Hell, I just sublet the basement to a Teasip."

Did you hear about the Mibbie who locked his keys in the car? It took him nine hours to get his family out.

Why did the Mibbie move his house five feet from its old foundation?
Because there was slack in his clothesline.

Did you hear about the Mibbie who cut correspondence school?
He sent in empty envelopes.

Then there was the Mibbie who threw himself on the floor and missed, and was so stupid that other Mibbies noticed.

Mibbie: "I just got a bicycle for my girl friend."
Second Mibbie: "How did you get such a good trade?"

Did you hear about the Mibbie who, when he heard his wife was going to have twins, went out looking for the other guy?
One day a Mibbie came home to find his wife in bed with an Aggie. In a fit of grief the Mibbie took out a gun and placed it to his temple.
The Aggie, feeling remorseful, said, "Hey, buddy, don't feel so upset ... this kind of thing happens all the time. Have a beer and forget it."
The Mibbie, with the gun still at his head said, "Shut up, stupid ... *you're next!*"

Then there was a Mibbie whose wife asked him to change the baby. He showed up an hour or so later with another child. But he was to be pitied: according to what his friends say, this Mibbie's wife had legs so hairy her knees had bangs. And when she cooked, she tended to burn the meat so badly they had to check dental records to see what they were eating.

Did you hear about the Mibbie who willed his body to science? Science is contesting the will.

Did you hear about the four Mibbies in a pickup truck which went into a canal? The two in the front were saved, but the two in back were lost because the tailgate was stuck.

Then there was a Mibbie who put on one boot because the weather forecaster called for only one foot of snow.

"Don't you ever peel the banana before eating it?" said the man to the Mibbie.
"No. I already know what's inside."

Then there was the Mibbie football star who when he got his varsity letter had to have his girl friend read it to him.

How many Mibbies does it take to eat a rabbit dinner?
Three. One to feast, and one to watch in each direction for cars.

Then there was the Mibbie who tried to have his marriage annulled when he found out her father had no license for the gun.

A Mibbie first smells his right armpit and smiles, then smells his left and frowns. "What's going on?" says a passerby. The Mibbie replies, "They haven't invented Left Guard yet."

Then there was the absentminded Mibbie professor

who forgot to write a twenty-five-dollar introductory text to sell his students.

Then there was the Mibbie who tried to trade his wife's menstrual cycle in on a new Honda.

Two Mibbies were building a house. One, examining each nail as he picked it up, was tossing about half of them away.

"What's the matter?" said the second Mibbie.

"About half of these nails have the head on the wrong end."

"You fool, those are for the other side of the house."

2. Funistradans

Ethnic insult jokes are perennial and over time tend to become omnidirectional. What is a Polish joke in Chicago is a Norwegian joke in Minneapolis, a "Newfie" joke in Toronto, a Tasmanian joke in Canberra, and an Irish joke in Boston. One group that has not gotten equal time in all of this are the witless Funistradans.* Their time has come.

How much does a Funistradan pay for a haircut?
   Four dollars—a buck for each side.

What do you call a man walking around with his
   hands in the air?
   A Funistradan on war maneuvers.

Why are Funistradan mothers so strong?
   It comes from raising dumbbells.

*It was argued by psychologist Jeffrey H. Goldstein in *Human Behavior* magazine that this kind of joke loses its punch if a fictitious nationality is used. The example he used were East Frisians. For this very reason I have shied away from a silly, fictitious nationality and will take my lumps for maligning Funistradans. If you have trouble finding it in your atlas, it is right next to Galubria.

What's this? (Asked with one's arms folded across
   one's chest.)
   A Funistradan bra.

Do you know the difference between a Funistradan
   wedding and a Funistradan funeral?
   There's one less drunk at a Funistradan funeral.

Why do flies have wings?
   To beat Funistradans to the garbage pails.

What is a group of Funistradan paratroopers called?
   Air pollution.

Who shot Mussolini eight times?
   Five hundred Funistradan sharpshooters.

How do Funistradans propose?
   You're going to have a what?

What has an IQ of 192?
   Funistrada.

How can you spot a Funistradan airplane?
   It has hair under its wings.

Why aren't Funistradans allowed to play bingo?
   They eat the corn.

What are twenty Funistradans lying on a lawn?
   Fertilizer.

What's the easiest job in the world?
   The head of Funistradan Intelligence.

What is gross stupidity?
   One hundred forty-four Funistradans.

What do you have when you extend your little fin-
   ger?

A Funistradan handkerchief.

What did the Funistradan do when he won an Olympic gold medal?
He had it bronzed.

Do you know why Funistradans only get half an hour off for lunch?
If they had an hour, they'd have to retrain him.

How does a Funistradan grease his car?
He runs over a Galubrian.

How does a Funistradan fan himself?
Holds his hand still and waves his face in front of it.

Why is Santa Claus Funistradan?
Who else would wear a red suit during the holidays?

Why don't they let Funistradans operate elevators?
They forget the route.

How many Funistradans does it require to take a picture off the wall?
Ten, one to hold the picture and nine to knock down the wall.

How can you tell where a rich flamingo lives?
By the wrought-iron Funistradans on the front lawn.

What happened when the Funistradan put snow tires on his car?
They melted.

How can you tell when a Funistradan has passed
   away?
   The garbage trucks go around with their lights on.

What does it say on the bottom of Coke bottles in
   Funistrada?
   Open other end.

How does a Funistradan spell *farm*?
   Ei-yi-ei-yi-o.

How do you make a Funistradan shish kebab?
   Shoot an arrow into a garbage can.

Why does one occasionally see Funistradans push-
   ing a house down the street?
   That's how they jump-start their furnaces.

Why don't Funistradan mothers nurse their babies?
   It hurts too much to boil their nipples.

Why do Funistradans have scratched faces on Monday morning?
   Because they eat with knives and forks over the
   weekend.

Why are Funistradan jokes so simple?
   So the Galubrians can understand them.

What is green, red, orange, chartreuse, purple,
   brown, pink, and covered with polka dots?
   A Funistradan woman dressed up for church.

What would happen if all the Funistradans in Chicago jumped into Lake Michigan?
   Lake Michigan would end up with a ring around
   it.

What constitutes a traditional Funistradan seven-
course dinner?
A can of sardines and a six-pack.

What is the smallest building in all of Funistrada?
The Hall of Fame.

How did the prime minister of Funistrada deal with
the problem of Red China?
He bought a pink tablecloth.

Did you hear about the border dispute between
the Funistradans and the Galubrians?
The Funistradans are throwing sticks of dynamite
across the border and the Galubrians are lighting
them and throwing them back.

How do Funistradan fishermen count their catch?
One fish ... two fish ... another fish ... another
fish ... another fish.

How does a Funistradan admiral review his fleet?
Through a glass-bottomed boat.

How does the account of a Funistradan wedding
party begin?
Among the injured were ...

Why do Funistradans stand up and smile when
there is lightning?
They think their pictures are being taken.

One Funistradan meets another on a road and notices that he has a bag of fried chicken. "Can I have
some?" he asks.
"Why should I give you any?"
"Okay. If I can guess how many you have in the
sack, could I have some?"
"If you can guess how many chickens are in here,"

says the second man, "you can have both of them."
"Three," says the first man.

A Funistradan, a Swede, and an Italian were passing a particularly smelly pigsty and decided to
have a contest to see who could stay in the sty the
longest. After five minutes the Italian came out, after
ten the Swede came out, and after twenty minutes
the pigs came out.

3. State of the Art

It broke out in the early 1980s and the biggest con-
flicts were reported regularly. "Insults and bitter barbs
are the ammunition of the Great Midwestern Joke War
now raging between Iowa and Minnesota," said the
Los Angeles Times in late 1982, while *USA Today* pro-
claimed that it was breaking out wherever there is "any
kind of regional identity." Examples carefully collected
to insult the residents of at least half the states:

Who has a beard, wears a dirty white robe, and rides
a pig?
Lawrence of Arkansas.

Why is it impossible to walk across New Jersey?
Nobody can hold his nose for that long.

Why are there no active volcanoes in California?
There are no virgins to sacrifice.

What is progress in Florida?
Separate electric chairs for smokers and non-smok-
ers.

What do they call an Oklahoman with indoor plumbing?
Kinky.

What's the difference between North Dakota and yogurt?
Yogurt has culture.

What do they call a handsome, intelligent man in
New Hampshire?
A tourist.

What do they call anybody with an IQ of ninety in
Louisiana?
Governor.

Did you hear about the Iowan who was killed in a
pie-eating contest?
The cow sat on him.

Did you hear that they had to close down the Georgia State Library?
Somebody stole the book.

What do they call the alphabet in Indiana?
The impossible dream.

What is the last thing a Kansas stripper takes off?
Her bowling shoes.

What do they say in Tennessee when a manure silo
falls over?
Shoot the looters.

What do they call a 1954 Buick in Alabama?
The bridal suite.

What do you call two dirty teddy bears and a tractor
that won't start?
The Maine State Fair.

What do you call a place with ten thousand lakes,
five thousand swamps, and one fish?

Minnesota.

How did the man from Wisconsin break his arm raking leaves?
He fell out of the tree.

Why did they have to remove the speed bumps from the roads in Kentucky?
People were doing their laundry on them.

What's the most popular television show in Montana?
90 Minutes—they have to slow it down so people can follow it.

Why do New Mexicans drink less Kool-Aid than folks in other states?
Because they have such a hard time getting two quarts of water into that little envelope.

Why do they have artificial turf at the University of Nebraska stadium?
So the cheerleaders won't graze at halftime.

How does a Texan tell the milkman he wants extra cottage cheese?
He pins a note to his wife's bra.

♪   ♪   ♪   ♪

4. Take That

One of the oldest forms of personal insult is the kind that turns on the word *that*.* Here is an introductory selection:

---

*Lest there be any confusion, *that* jokes are applied not only to individuals; for instance, "It was so cold in Chicago that I saw an alderman with his hands in his own pocket," or 'This town was so small that the town slut was a virgin."

He was so vain that he had his X rays retouched.

Her life was so dull that she looked forward to dental appointments.

He was so mean that he enjoyed reading Horatio Alger books backwards.

She was so dumb that she thought a buttress was a female goat.

He was so dull that his dog got bored and left him.

Her luck was so bad that her contacts got cataracts.

He was so dumb that he couldn't tell you which way an elevator was going if you gave him three guesses.

She was so knock-kneed and he was so bowlegged that when they stood together they spelled *OX*.

He was so nervous that he kept coffee awake.

She was so ugly that when she walked into a room the mice jumped on a chair.

His feet were so big that he had to put his pants on over his head.

She was so cheap that she only did crossword puzzles vertically so that she wouldn't have to come across.

He was so lazy that he married a pregnant woman.

He was so rich that the Joneses try to keep up with him.

She had such bony legs that when she sat down, her knees made a fist.

He was so dumb that when he rented a room the landlady left the VACANT sign up.

She was so thin that when she wore a fur coat she looked like a pipe cleaner.

He was so thin that when he closed one eye he could pass for a needle.

She had been married so many times that she had rice marks on her face.

He was so dumb that he had to ask his wife to take her sweater off to count to two.

She was so unattractive that she had to get BO to attract attention.

She was so rich that she sent her dishes out to be dry-cleaned.

He was so cheap that he ate beans to save money on bubblebath.

Her nose was so upturned that every time she sneezed, she blew her hat off.

He was so fat that he had to make two trips when he left the house.

She spent so much time in parked cars that they are now showing her on some road maps.

He was so dumb he thought a Band-Aid was a charitable organization for musicians.

She was so cheap that she used only one ice cube when she had a headache.

He was so cheap that he wouldn't even tip in a canoe.

She had so many double chins that she could wear a string of pearls without the string.

He was so slow that they had to show him how the wastebasket worked the first day on his new job.

She was so dumb that she thought the Pied Piper was a drunken plumber.

He was so self-conscious that when he went to a football game and the players went into a huddle; he thought they were talking about him.

She was so thin that when she swallowed an olive three men left town.

He was so cross-eyed that when he cried, the tears from his left eye landed on his right cheek.

She was so ugly that when she was a child her parents always took her along so that they wouldn't have to say good-bye.

He was so fat that he could only play seek.

She was so dumb that she thought you had to take music lessons to fiddle around.

He was so dumb that the fortune-teller read his mind for half price.

She was so dumb that she thought Alexander Haig was a drink made of Scotch and milk.

His breath was so bad that they pushed him over three times last Halloween.

She was so dumb that she thought *Forever Amber* was a stalled traffic light.

He was so dumb that he thought Einstein was one beer.

She was so dumb that she thought Eartha Kitt was an Italian gardening set.

His nose was so big that he could smoke a cigar in the shower.

She was such a prude that she blushed when someone said "intersection."

He was so crooked that he could stand in the shadow of a corkscrew.

She was so cross-eyed that she thought the sun set in the east.

He was so crooked that when he pulled the wool over your eyes it was fifty percent polyester.

She was so dumb that she saw a sign that said Murderer Wanted and she applied for the job.

Eternal Questions

Undoubtedly there are other answers to these questions, but there are limits.

I

What's black and white and red all over?
- A newspaper.
- A skunk in a blender.
- *Pravda.*
- Two prostitutes standing outside an integrated brothel.
- Santa Claus coming down the chimney.
- A chocolate sundae with ketchup on it.
- An English setter with mange.
- A penguin with the measles.
- A wounded nun.
- A blushing zebra.
- A sunburned penguin.
- A skunk with diaper rash.
- Students for a Democratic Society (an answer from the 1960s).

II

"Who was that lady I saw you with last night?"
   "That was no lady, that was my wife."

"Who was that lady I saw you with last night?"
"That was no lady. That was your wife."

"Who was that lady I saw you with last night?"
"That was no lady, that was my wife."
"Don't be silly. *I'm your wife.*"

"Who was that lady I saw you out with last night?"
"I wasn't out, I was just dozing."

"Who was that lady I seen you with last night?"
"You mean, 'I saw.' "
"Okay—who was that eyesore I seen you with last night?"

"Who was that lady I saw you with last night?"
"That was no lady, that was a grapefruit—when I squeezed her she hit me in the eye."

"Who was that lady I saw you out wit' last night?"
"Who said I could outwit a lady?"

Lancelot to Guinevere: "Who was that last knight I saw you out with, Lady?"

Cain: "Who was that lady I saw you out with last night?"
Adam: "That wasn't night, that was Eve."

First Cannibal: "Who was that lady I saw you with last night?"
Second Cannibal: "That was no lady, that was my lunch."

"Who was that gentlemen I saw you with last night?"
"That was no gentleman. That was a senator."

"Who was that wench I saw you with last night?"
"That was no wench, that was my hammer."

Magician to woman assistant:
"Who was that lady I sawed you with last night?"
"That was no lady—that was my half-sister."

III

"Why did the chicken cross the road?"
  "To get to the other side."

"Why did the chicken cross the road?"
  "Because it was a fowl proceeding."

"Why does the chicken step over the wheel rut?"
  "Because it's too far to walk around."

"Why did the hen stop in the middle of the road?"
  "She wanted to lay it on the line."

"Why didn't the elephant cross the road?"
  "He didn't want to be mistaken for a chicken."

"Why did the otter cross the road?"
  "To get to the otter side."

"Why did the unwashed chicken cross the road
  twice?"
  "Because it was a dirty double-crosser."

"Why did the chicken cross the road?"
  "To get Social Security."
  (You don't get it? Well, neither did the chicken;
  she wasn't 65.)

"Why did the cow cross the road?"
  "Because it was the chicken's day off."

"Why don't you ever see chickens in the zoo?"
  "Because they can't afford the admission."

IV

Have you ever seen a horse fly?
  No.
  Have you ever seen:
  An egg box?
  A uniform smile?

A stone step?
A boardwalk?
A ball park?
A key punch?
A hot dog stand?
A shoe box?
A square dance?
A picket fence?
A ginger snap?
A fire fly?
A king fish?
A home run?
A salad bowl?
A tree bark?
A hog bristle?

V

What do you get when you cross . . .

. . . a lion and a parrot?
  I don't know, but when it talks you'd better listen.

. . . a cat with a lemon?
  A sour puss.

. . . a turtle and a cow?
  A turtleneck jersey.

. . . a bumblebee with a doorbell?
  A hum dinger.

. . . a pig and a billy goat?
  A crashing boar.

. . . stripteaser with a tropical fruit?
  A self-peeling banana.

. . . an eel and a jellyfish?
  Currant jelly.

. . . a kangaroo and a raccoon?
  A fur coat with pockets.

. . . a zebra and a whale?
A traffic jam.

. . . an owl and a goat?
A hootennany.

. . . an elephant with a jar of peanut butter?
You either get peanut butter with a wonderful
memory or an elephant that sticks to the roof of
your mouth.

. . . a pig, a pool table, and a tall tree?
A pork-cue-pine.

. . . a chicken with a waitress?
A chicken that lays tables.

. . . a fish and an elephant?
Swimming trunks.

. . . a centipede and a turkey?
Drumsticks for everyone.

. . . a crocodile and an abalone?
A crock-abalone.

. . . porcupine with a sheep?
An animal that knits its own sweaters.

. . . sheep with a kangaroo?
A woolen jumper.

. . . a pile of hay and a vampire?
A bale o' Lugosi.

. . . a boa constrictor and pasta?
Spaghetti that winds itself around the fork.

. . . an elephant and a kangaroo?
Potholes all over Australia.

. . . a stripper and a vegetarian?
A woman who doesn't want dressing on her salad.

. . . a gorilla and a mink?
A fur coat with sleeves that are too long.

... a flea with a rabbit?
A bug's bunny.

... a hen with a banjo?
A self-plucking chicken.

... a dentist, a manicurist, and a soldier?
Someone who fights tooth and nail.

... a manicurist and a chiropodist?
Someone who waits on you hand and foot.

... fifty thousand pigth and fifty thousand deerth?
One hundred thows and buckth.

... an undertaker and a snake charmer?
Don't know, but it has hiss and hearse towels.

... a shark and a parrot?
An animal that will talk your ear off.

... a goat and an eel?
An electric can opener.

... a dog and a chicken?
A pooched egg.

... poison ivy and a four-leaf clover?
A rash of good luck.

... the side of your head with an angry little girl?
Surly Temple.

VI

What has four legs and flies?
- A picnic table.
- A dead horse.
- Two pairs of pants.

Martians, Panhandlers, and a Few Cannibals

Certain joke characters set up such great situations that their joke popularity is all out of proportion to reality. The stars of this chapter—the Martian, the panhandler, and the cannibal—make the point in the extreme. The Martian is fiction, there are very few panhandlers these days (save for the airport variety), and there is no firm evidence to indicate that there ever were such things as true cannibal tribes.

1. Martians

They existed before 1957, but they got their big push in October of that year when the Soviet Union put its Sputnik I into orbit. The Space Age had begun and a new joke fad was called for.

The first thing a Martian looks for after arriving on earth is a men's room. He finds one and, on the way out the door, notices the paper towel dispenser.

"Lady," he says, "your slip is showing."

"Are you from Mars?" he asked the green man with six arms.

"Yes."

"Are you all green with six arms?"

"Yes."

"Do you all have antennas sticking out of your head?"

"Yes."

"Do you all have little black caps on top of your head?"

"Only the orthodox."

A one-foot tall Martian lands on earth and the first person he encounters is a beautiful six-foot-tall woman.

"Take me to your ladder, lady: I'll see your leader later."

What did the Martian say to the tomcat?
"Take me to your litter."
. . . to the supermarket manager?
"Take me to your Liederkranz."
. . . to the forest ranger who has found him in a pile of leaves?
"Rake me to your leader."

During Eisenhower's presidency, a Martian landed on the White House lawn dressed in a vicuña coat and said to the Secret Service man who came out to meet him, "Lead me to your taker."

A little green man pops out of a flying saucer on Pennsylvania Avenue, walks up to Vice-President — —and says, "Take me to your leader."

The Vice-President replies, "Don't be ridiculous. I hardly know the man!"

(This has been applied to every Vice-President since Humphrey.)

Late at night two newly arrived Martians walked up Second Avenue in New York eating garbage cans.

"You know," said one, "the crusts are good, but the filling is too rich for me."

"She's not only beautiful, but she's got brains," said the Martian after seeing his first computer.

Two Martians land in Las Vegas and pass a slot machine which suddenly disgorges a load of silver dollars.

One Martian turns to the other and says, "He's foolish not to be home with a cold like that."

A Martian lands in a small town, walks into a sleazy bar, and is immediately attracted to its garish jukebox. "What's a nice girl like you doing in a joint like this?"

The Martian scout lands his spaceship at a gas station that is closed. He walks up to the first pump and says, "I am friendly. Take me to your leader." Getting no answer, he goes to the next pump and still gets no answer. After trying all the pumps, he walks back to his spacecraft and returns to Mars.

Upon arriving home, he reports to his chief, "These earthlings are terrible. They are rude and unsociable and I couldn't get a word out of them. But boy, are they hung!"

An earth couple is carried away to Mars by a Martian spaceship. After landing they are told that no harm will be done to them, but that the only reason they were abducted was to study them. After a cordial day of questioning, the Martian leader says, "I think we're just about done with you, but we have one final request: could you show us how you get your babies?"

After much self-conscious hemming and hawing the couple decide that they should perform for the sake of interplanetary understanding.

When they have finished, the Martian leader says, "How disappointing!"

"Why?" say the couple in unison.

"Because that's how we make automobiles."

"Isn't she beautiful?" said the Martian as he approached a snazzy new motor scooter. "I think I'll take her back to Mars with us."

"Watch what you're doing," his partner warned. "She may be underage."

A Martian couple walk by a hardware store and the female stops to admire the paint cans in the window.

"I'm sorry," says the man, "your old coat will have to last you another year."

Two Martians land and first encounter a television set. They turn it on and begin to watch a western.

"This is fascinating," says the first Martian to the second, "but what I can't figure out is why the hero has a biped on his back."

A Martian noticed an apartment building covered with television aerials. "Hey, kids," he yelled, "get down from there before you hurt yourselves."

Moments after the Martian has landed on earth a large truck passes him and drops a big box on the road.

"Lady, lady," he yells, "you dropped your purse."

A Martian lands in downtown Chicago and walks over to a traffic light and says sympathetically, "Gee, pal, you must have had a rough night."

A Martian spaceship lands in The Bronx and the impact of landing is so great that the wheels on the craft are destroyed.

Two Martians set out to find replacement wheels and to their great relief immediately encounter a store with a large assortment of wheels in the window.

"We'll take four of those wheels in the window," says one of the Martians to the shopkeeper.

"Those aren't wheels," he says. "They're bagels. They're to eat—here, try one."

The two Martians take a few bites and then one turns to the shopkeeper and says, "They aren't bad, but they'd be a lot better with cream cheese and lox."

Several Martians disguised as humans land in New York City and head straight for a fancy restaurant for lunch.

At the end of the meal the waiter says to them, "You guys must be Martians."

"How did you know?" says the Martian chief.

"You're the only people who've paid cash in the last six months."

A Martian who has just landed is approached by a panhandler who says, "Can you spare a dime, mister?"

"What's a dime?" says the Martian.

"You're right. Make it a quarter."

2. Panhandlers

The old panhandler living in New York hears that his brother is very sick in Los Angeles. By working day and night for a week he is able to beg enough money to buy his airline ticket. He arrives at Kennedy Airport, goes to the ticket counter, and plunks down all the money. The clerk at the counter counts the money and says to the man, "I'm sorry sir, but you're a nickel short."

The panhandler tells the clerk that he'll be right back. He runs out in front of the terminal and stops the first man he sees.

"Mister, can you let me have a nickel so I can get to California?"

The stranger flips him a quarter and says, "Here—take four of your friends."

"Mister, would you be kind enough to let me have fifty dollars?"

"What gall! What made you think that you could ask for so much?"

"Well, I just thought I'd put all my begs in one ask it."

"Mister, will you give me a buck for a sandwich?"

"Let's see the sandwich."

"Mister, will you give me three hundred dollars for a cup of coffee?"

"Three hundred dollars?"

"Yes, to go to Brazil—I like it fresh."

"Mister, have you enough for a cup of coffee?"

"Oh, I'll manage somehow, thanks."

"Mister, can you give me a bite?"

"You're too dirty to bite."

"Mister, could you spare seven-fifty for a cup of coffee?"

"Seven-fifty for a cup of coffee? That's preposterous."

"Just give me a yes or no, don't tell me how to run my business."

"Mister, I haven't tasted food in a week."

"Don't worry, it still tastes the same."

"Mister, can I have a hundred twenty-five dollars for a cup of coffee?"

"A hundred twenty-five dollars?"

"Well, I couldn't go into a restaurant dressed like this."

"Mister, can I have a quarter?"

"Of all the nerve! How dare you stop people on the street and ask for money?"

"What do you want me to do, open an office?"

"Mister, can I have twenty dollars for a cup of coffee?"
"Twenty dollars for a cup of coffee?"
"Can I help it if I'm a big tipper?"

"Mister, can I have a dime for a cup of . . . Forget that line. I'll be honest with you. I'm saving up for a double shot of whiskey."
"I'll be just as honest with you," the man replied. "I'm saving up for a new car."

"Mister," said the panhandler, holding out two hats, "can I have some money?"
"Okay, but why two hats?"
"Well, sir, business has been so good that I decided to open a branch office."

A man sees an old panhandler and addresses him: "Why don't you get a job, save your money, then invest it? Then you will become rich like me and not have to work anymore."
"Why should I go to all that trouble?" said the panhandler. "I'm not working now."

"Mister, how about a quarter for a cup of coffee?"
Good Samaritan: "My good man, here's seventy-five cents for three cups."
The next morning the same panhandler approaches the good Samaritan.
"Are you the guy who gave me seventy-five cents for three cups of coffee last night?"
"Yes."
"Well, drop dead—I couldn't sleep a wink all night."

"Mister, how about some money for a cup of coffee?"
"Money for coffee," the man yelled back. "Just look at yourself—a dirty, smelly wreck of a man. But I'm

willing to help you. I'll get you cleaned and properly clothed and well fed on the condition that you get a handle on yourself and find a job."

The panhandler looked at the man with astonishment. "Go to work? What for, to support a bum like me?"

"Lady, could you spare me two bits so I can buy something to eat?"

"Why are you begging—a big, strong man like yourself? You should be ashamed."

"Madam," says the panhandler, removing his hat and bowing low, "I am an incurable romantic. I have woven lovely dreams and the wind has swept them away. And so I have turned to this profession—the only one in which a man can approach a beautiful, generous woman like yourself without being introduced."

"I haven't eaten in three days, could you let me have a penny?"

"What can you do with a penny?"

"I'm very anxious to weigh myself."

Woman: "Are you really content to spend your life walking around begging?"

Panhandler: "No, lady—many's the time I've wished I had a car."

"Here's a dime for you, my poor man," said the gentleman to the panhandler, adding, "Tell me, please, how did you get yourself into this state of poverty?"

"I was always like you, mister—giving away vast sums to the poor and needy."

"Lady, could you help a poor blind man?"

"How do I know you're blind?"

"How do I know you're a lady?"

"Lady, please help me. I haven't eaten for four days."

"Gracious me, I certainly wish I had your willpower."

"I should think you would be ashamed to beg in this neighborhood," said the well-dressed man to the panhandler.

"Don't apologize, sir," replied the panhandler. "I've seen worse."

"Okay, Okay," said the man to the panhandler, "I'll give you some money—a dime—if you'll tell me what you are going to do with it."

"Well, sir, first I'll buy the finest meal in town, replete with the rarest wine, then I will purchase a brand-new car, and at this point there should be enough left to put the down payment on a home in one of our better suburbs."

The man drew a quarter from his pocket and handed it to the panhandler. "Take this, my friend, and live in happiness for the remainder of your days."

"Sir, can you give me some change? I'm very hungry."

"I'd love to, but I don't have a cent with me. However, I am going to the bank and I'd be glad to meet you here in an hour and give you enough for a hot meal."

"I can't do that," said the panhandler. "Do you realize how much I lose giving credit?"

A panhandler stopped a man on the street and asked for a buck with which to buy a sandwich.

"Listen," said the man, "I'll give you two bucks if you'll answer a question: Do you drink, smoke, gamble, or run around with wicked women?"

"I've never done any of those things" was his quick reply.

"All right, if you'll come home with me I'll make it five bucks."

As the man walked in the door with the bedraggled panhandler, his wife asked, "What's this?"

"This, my dear, is what happens to a man who

doesn't drink, smoke, gamble, or run around with
wicked women."

3. Cannibals

"Why don't you come to my house for dinner tonight?" said the first cannibal. "We're having my
mother-in-law."

"I don't like your mother-in-law," said the second.

"All right, then just come for dessert and coffee."

Trying to prove that even cannibalism can be cured,
a noted psychologist takes one of the world's most notorious cannibals and puts him through five years of
intense treatment and civilized schooling at a first-rate
university.

After curing him totally, the psychologist tours with
the man for a year to show what has been accomplished. At the end of the year the psychologist realizes
that the man is in need of a vacation so he buys him
passage on an ocean cruise.

The first day he is sitting in the dining salon and the
steward asks, "Would you like to see our menu?"

"No—the passenger list."

"Yes," said the cannibal after dinner, "my wife makes
good soup, but I'm sure going to miss her."

"It's like lobster," said the cannibal mother to her
child on seeing his first airliner, "you only eat what's
inside."

Did you hear about the cannibal student who was
suspended from school for buttering up his teacher?
And then there was the cannibal chief's daughter who
liked boys best when they were stewed. And then there
was the beatnik cannibal who ate three squares a day.

"Yes," said the cannibal king, "everyone's eaten."

What's the Difference?

They are really hybrids—part pun and part riddle—and are among the oldest of formulas showing up in the most ancient joke and riddle books. They invariably begin with the phrase "What's the difference between . . ." and fall into two natural groups, innocent and not so innocent. Those of the latter group usually feature only half an answer, since the second half of the answer is usually painfully obvious. For instance, "What's the difference between a cactus and a caucus?" "The pricks are on the outside of a cactus." Selection from both groups:

I

What's the difference between a light in a cave and a dance at an inn?

One is a taper in a cavern, the other is a caper in a tavern.

What's the difference between Christopher Columbus and the lid of a dish?

One is a discoverer, and the other is a dish coverer.

What's the difference between a riddle and a man's aunt who squints?

One is a query with an answer, the other an aunt, sir, with a queer eye.

What's the difference between your granny and your granary?

One is your born kin, the other is your cornbin.

What's the difference between the crown prince, an orphan, a baldheaded old man, and a mama gorilla?

One is an heir apparent, one has ne'er a parent, one no hair apparent, and one a hairy parent.

What's the difference between a chess player and a man who is broke?

One watches his pawn; the other pawns his watch.

What's the difference between your last will and testament and a man who has eaten as much as he can?

One's signed and dated, the other dined and sated.

What's the difference between a tenant and the son of a widow?

The tenant has to pay rents, but the son of a widow has not two parents.

What's the difference between a summer dress in winter and an extracted molar?

One is too thin, the other tooth out.

What's the difference between an auction and sea-sickness?

One is the sale of effects, the other the effects of a sail.

What's the difference between last week's *Newsweek* and the brewings of Guinness and Molson?

One is out and stale, the others stout and ale.

What's the difference between a photocopy machine and the Hong Kong flu?

The one makes facsimiles, the other sick families.

What's the difference between a land surveyor and an ascot?

One is agent for property, the other a proper tie for a gent.

What's the difference between a cloud and a boy getting a spanking?

The cloud pours with rain and the boy roars with pain.

What's the difference between an organist and a cold in the head?

One knows the stops, and the other stops the nose.

What's the difference between a barber and a woman with many children?

One has razors to shave, and the other has shavers to raise.

What's the difference between a crazy hare and a counterfeit coin?

One is a mad bunny, and the other is bad money.

What's the difference between a cat and a comma?

The cat has claws at the end of his paws, while the comma has its pause at the end of its clause.

What's the difference between a sailor and six broken clocks?

The sailor goes to sea, and the clocks cease to go.

What's the difference between a fisherman and a lazy schoolboy?

One baits his hook, while the other hates his book.

What's the difference between a buffalo and a bison?

You can't wash your hands in a buffalo.

What's the difference between a person who tries to hit all the seagulls with a rock and the person who tries to paint all the backsides of baboons?

One tries to leave no tern unstoned and the other tries to leave no stern untoned.

What's the difference between a dog losing his hair and a man painting a small building?

One is shedding his coat, and the other is coating his shed.

What's the difference between an apple and a pretty girl?

The one you squeeze to get cider, the other you get 'side 'er to squeeze.

What's the difference between a gardener, a billiard player, a precise man, and a church janitor?

The gardener minds his peas; the billiard player his cues; the precise man, his p's and q's; and the church janitor, his keys and pews.

What's the difference between Noah's ark and Joan of Arc?

Noah's ark was made of wood and Joan of Arc was maid of Orleans. And now tell me the difference between Joan of Arc and Queen Elizabeth?

Joan of Arc was a wonder, and Queen Elizabeth was a Tudor.

What's the difference between a man going to the second floor and a man looking upstairs?

One is stepping upstairs, and the other is staring up steps.

What's the difference between a china shop and a furniture store?

One sells tea sets, while the other sells settees.

What is the difference between a duck with one wing and one with two?

A difference of a pinion.

What's the difference between an old penny and a new dime?

Nine cents.

II

What's the difference between a bad marksman and a constipated owl?

A bad marksman shoots and shoots and never hits.

What's the difference between a rooster and a lawyer?

A rooster clucks defiance.

What's the difference between a seagull and a baby?

A seagull flits along the shore.

What's the difference between a eunuch and an Eskimo?

A eunuch is a massive vassal with a passive tassel, while an Eskimo is a rigid midget with a frigid digit.

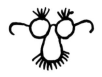

A School of Heard Knocks

A basic repertoire of knock-knocks guaranteed to get you through a rainy afternoon at the beach, whether it be in the company of Cub Scouts or Ph.D.'s.

So that a fairly large selection could be presented here, the first three lines have been eliminated from each knock-knock. Under normal circumstances this is unpardonable and I promise not to do it again. Also, the reader must hereby promise never to abbreviate the spoken knock-knock ritual. To do so is to rob it of its sophistication and actually make the jokes sound silly.

Adolph who?
  Adolph ball hit me in the head. That's why I talk like this.

Alby who?
  Alby glad when you're dead, you rascal you.

Alfred who?
  Alfred the needle if you'll sew on the button.

Agatha who?
  Agatha feeling you're foolin'.

Amis who?
  Amis is as good as a mile.

Amos who?
  Amos-quito bit me.

Amsterdam who?

Amsterdam tired of these knock-knocks, I could scream.

Andy who?
  Andy bit me again.

Apollo who?
  Apollo you anywhere if you'll blow in my ear.

Ardyth who?
  Ardyth da thpeech therapy offith?

Arthur who?
  Arthur any more at home like you?

Arthur who?
  Arthur mometer is broken.

Artis who?
  Artis in the eye of the beholder.

Atch who?
  Gesundheit.

Avenue who?
  Avenue heard this knock-knock joke before?

The Avon lady, who?
  Your doorbell's broken.

Barcelona who?
  My sister doesn't go to Barcelona.

Ben Hur who?
  Ben Hur an hour and she ain't in sight.

Black Panther who?
  Black Panther what I wear. What do you wear?

Butch, Jimmy, and Joe who?
  Butch your arms around me, Jimmy a kiss, or I'll Joe home.

Cairo who?
  Cairo the boat now?

Cameron who?

Cameron film are what you need to take pictures.

Canoe who?
Canoe come out and play?

Cargo who?
Cargo beep, beep.

Celeste who?
Celeste time I'll ask you.

Centipede who?
Centipede on the Christmas tree.

Chester who?
Chester minute and I'll see.

Cigar who?
Cigarlette fever.

Cigarette who?
Cigarette agent.

Cigarette who?
Cigarette life if you don't weaken.

Cirrhosis who?
Cirrhosis red and violets are blue.

Conrad who?
Conrad the whole book.

Curtis who?
Curtis Interruptus.

Curtis who?
Curtis see is contagious.

Dandelion who?
Isn't it dandelion around all day doing nothing?

Deep who?
Deep ends on who you were expecting.

Delores who?
Delores be an England

Dennis who?
Dennis the room where I keep my books.

Descartes who?
  Don't put Descartes before the horse.

Dictaphone who?
  Dictaphone back on the receiver and stop running
  up my bill.

Don Giovanni who?
  Don Giovanni any ice cream today?

Doughnut who?
  Doughnut open until Christmas.

Eisenhower who?
  Eisenhower late for work.

Emerson who?
  Emerson nice shoes you've got on.

Event who?
  Event that-a-way.

Eyewash who?
  Eyewash I had a million dollars.

Flo who?
  Flo ride is good for your teeth.

Formaldehyde who?
  Formaldehyden places came the hostile Indians.

Frankie who?
  Frankie, Scarlett, I don't give a damn!

Gibbon who?
  Gibbon take if you want to get along in the world.

Gus who?
  Gus who's coming for dinner.

Hence who?
  Hence lay eggs.

Henrietta and Juliet who?
  Henrietta big dinner and got sick, Juliet the same
  thing, but she's okay.

A herd who?
  A herd you were home, so I came over!

Hewlett who?
  Hewlett the cat out of the bag?

Howard who?
  Howard you today?

Howie who?
  Fine, thanks, Howie you?

Howie who?
  Howie going to get into the movie with no money?

Gunga Din who?
  Gunga Din for free, 'cause I know the usher.

Hugh who?
  Hugh who to you, too.

Hutch who?
  God bless you.

Hyman who?
  Hyman, what's new and groovy?

Ira who?
  Ira member Mama.

Irish stew who?
  Irish stew in the name of the law.

Irving who?
  Irving a wonderful time, wish you were here.

Isabel who?
  Isabel necessary on a bicycle?

Jeeter who?
  Jeeter, get off the pot.

Just Diane who?
  Just Diane to see you.

Kleenex who?
Kleenex are prettier than dirty necks.

Little old lady who?
I didn't know you could yodel.

M. 'n O. who?
M. 'n O. gonna say.

Mandy who?
Mandy lifeboats.

Malcolm who?
Malcolm over to see me sometime.

Marion who?
Marion haste, repent at leisure.

Monopoly who?
Monopoly's bigger than your nopoly.

Moron who?
Moron the way, see below.

Morris who?
Morris Monday; next day's Tuesday.

Mortimer who?
Mortimer pitied than scorned.

Nixon who?
Nixon stones will break my bones.

Nona who?
Nona your business.

Norman who?
Norman nor beast should be out on a night like this.

Norway who?
There's Norway this knock-knock will work.

Oblong who?
Oblong Cassidy. You were expecting Roy Rogers maybe?

Oklahoma who?
Oklahoma wash your face.

Oliver who?
Oliver troubles will soon be over.

Osborn who?
Osborn in the state of Georgia.

Oswald who?
Oswald my gum.

Pecan who?
Pecan somebody your own size.

Polly Warner who?
Polly Warner cracker.

Popeye who?
Popeye've got to have the car tonight.

Radio who?
Radio not, here I come.

Sagittarius who?
Sagittarius State Schultz.

Salada who?
Salada bad knock-knock jokes going around.

Sarah who?
Sarah doctor in the house?

Sherwood who?
Sherwood like for you to let me in.

Statue who?
Statue in there?

Stephen who?
Stephen my toe and I'll holler.

Sweden who?
Sweden my tea with two lumps of sugar.

Tasmania who?
Tasmania slip 'twixt the cup and the lip.

Thelma who?
Thelma, Pretty Maiden, are there any more at
home like you?

Thesis who?
  Thesis a recording.

Thistle who?
  Thistle make you whistle.

Tijuana who?
  Tijuana play some baseball later?

Unawares who?
  Unawares what you put on first thing each morning.

Urdu who?
  She don't but her sister Urdu.

Urologist who?
  Urologist a bunch of nuts.

Vera who?
  Vera interesting.

Walter who?
  Walter wall carpet.

Winnie who?
  Winnie you going to think up a better joke?

Wren who?
  Wren are you coming out?

Yoda who?
  Yoda most forgettable person I ever met.

Yule who?
  Yule come on down, you hear?

Yvonne who?
  Yvonne to be alone.

Thistle who?
  Thistle be the last knock-knock joke.

Ménagerie à Trois

When this project began, I decided to apply one of the central organizing principles of my life, which is the *Tom Sawyer Whitewash Principle*. It comes from the famous incident in Mark Twain's *Adventures of Tom Sawyer* in which Tom got his pals to paint a fence with various subterfuges and lines like "Like it? Well, I don't see why I oughtn't to like it. Does a boy get to whitewash a fence every day?" Stated most concisely, the principle holds that if you tell enough people what fun you are having, a given number will line up for a piece of the action.

In this case I let all sorts of people, friends, acquaintances, and people I had never met but had corresponded with regarding other books of mine (and, in those cases where I applied the same principle, theirs) in on the fact that I was doing a jokebook—"Does a man," I asked, "get to brew up a jokebook every day?"—and I got all sorts of helpers. Some came across with a gem of a joke, while others sent a raft of them. It was not all as easy as it might sound: calls at odd hours to pass along a forty-year-old traveling-salesman joke, long letters crammed with old lines from *Captain Willie's Whiz Bang* (honest!), and more.

But a handful of these stalwarts went beyond the basic notion of a few pet jokes and offered a coherent collection of original-theme jokes. Curiously, 86.2 percent of these were based on animal and vegetable themes. Here are three of these remarkable collections, which also show that it is not only possible to get help painting a fence, but that some people will build a new section of fence for you.

I. Ofishal Puns

Cynthia MacGregor of New York accepts the blame for most of these:

1. Who's the famous fish with the pointing arm on the recruiting poster?
Uncle Salmon.

2. Why did the fish get turned down by the Army?
He failed his herring test.

3. How did the escargot cross the lake?
By snail boat.

4. Why did the crustacean divorce her husband?
He was an old crab.

5. How do you keep fish in jail?
With strong lox.

6. Ten fishermen had a great day's catch at a small lake. Who was the saddest fish that evening?
The sole survivor.

7. Who is the fish that always overeats?
Porgy pig.

8. How did the fish pay for expensive surgery?
He got a break on the price because he had a cousin who was a famous sturgeon.

9. What did the fisherman say to the magician?
Take a cod, any cod.

10. How does Mama Salmon differentiate among her offspring?

She arranges them roe by roe.

11. Why did the fish who was in a hurry hop on the back of another fish?

He knew he could travel faster on the pike.

12. Why didn't the fish want to make love?
He had a haddock.

13. What do fish sing on Sunday morning?
Nearer, my cod, to thee.

14. Why did the parakeet fly onto the fish's back?
He was looking for a perch.

15. Who defends the ocean from foreign invaders?
Sole-diers, snailors, and pilot fish.

16. Why did the minister spend so much time underwater?

He was interested in saving soles.

17. Ab and Eb were brothers. One day Momma fish got angry and yelled at Eb. Why?

Because Eb was a mean tease and he wouldn't leave Abalone.

18. What's the number-one song underwater?
"O Sole Mio."

Ms. MacGregor does not restrict her work to fish, as she sheepishly admits.

1. How does a sheep protect his driver's license?
He has it lamb-inated.

2. What's the sheep's favorite comic strip?
Mutton Jeff.

3. Where do sheep go when they want to barter?
To the five-and-ten because they know they'll get their Woolworth.

4. What do you read at a sheep funeral?
A lamb-ment.

5. Why were the Platters the sheep's favorite singing group?
Because one of their great hits was "Only Ewe."

6. What football team did the ewe cheer for?
No, not the rams! Navy, because she heard they kept everything sheep-shape.

II. An answer to the question: "How far can you run with one pun?"

Most people have heard this age-old question and answer:

What happened in the race between the lettuce, the faucet, and the tomato?
Lettuce was a head, faucet kept running, and tomato strained to ketchup.

Paul Zaslaw of Milton, Massachusetts, became concerned with the other participants in that race and posted these results:

GLUE	was fast paste
EGG	got cracking and scrambled away
MUG OF BEER	was only a chaser
KANGAROO	ran out of bounce
FLY	lost its zip
ODOMETER	was on the dash
STUDENT	was unable to make a high grade in the course

BANANA	peeled off fruitlessly
WATCH	wound down and eventually stopped running
TOILET PAPER	wiped out early
AUTHOR	was Swift
DECK OF CARDS	shuffled through
CHOCOLATE MILK	was Quik, but took an early spill
SHRUB	was a little bushed
SHOE	really stepped on it
PROSTITUTE	hustled through her opening lap
WHEEL	lost its bearings
INK	ran all over the place
JUNKIE	was caught speeding
CREDIT CARD	charged on
MANURE	covered a lot of ground
TELEPHONE	got hung up somewhere along the line
KNIFE	just couldn't cut it
CALENDAR	was observed only to March fourth
TAILOR	let out long pants and pressed on
CENTAUR	ran a half-assed race
STAIRCASE	took a flight
FOREIGNER	was Russian
PEN	started skipping
KING'S CHAIR	was throne, of course
SPERM CELL	petered out
PIPE	tried running with clogs, but was soon drained
SOAP DISH	was full of Zest
FROG	croaked along the way
BULLDOZER	tore up the road

NOSE	never stopped running
BICYCLE	was two-tired for racing
CHECK	bounced on a loan
GROCER	ran out of juice
DINNER JACKET ..	was worn out
PENCIL	was used to erase and lead to a point
NUT	turned and bolted
CANDLE	had a wicked start, but finally burned itself out
INVALID	passed on toward the end
WAVES	were not able to remain a wake
PLAYBOY	got behind early
RABBIT	hopped to it
TROUSERS	slacked off, but ran a fine overall race
WOOL	was on the lamb
VEGETABLE	was beet
LITTLE MISS MUFFET	lost her whey
DRESS	was just a long jumper
PAINT	started streaking

III. *The Case of the Five-Hundred-Pound Canary*

Martin S. Kottmeyer of Illinois wrote most of these ten years ago and claims he didn't want them unleashed on the world in these troubled times: but I convinced him that the world would be a better place if he let them out. To set the mood for this, Kottmeyer sent along a news clipping with the following lead paragraph:

500-POUND SPARROW ON LOOSE?
Casper, Wyo. (UPI)—A deputy investigating the

theft of 11 worms hopes a reward offered in the case won't produce any more tips like the one suggesting he question the nearest 500-pound sparrow.

What has four feet, four wings, four eyes, is yellow, and weighs half a ton?
  Two five-hundred-pound canaries.

Why do five-hundred-pound canaries have wings?
  So you can tell them from duckbill platypuses.

Why are five-hundred-pound canaries rare?
  Because a lot of people don't like them well done.

Why are five-hundred-pound canaries tough?
  Because they are so rare.

What should you look for when buying a five-hundred-pound canary?
  The Good Housekeeping Seal of Approval.

What should you look for when buying several five-hundred-pound canaries?
  A psychiatrist.
  Group insurance.

How do you lure a five-hundred-pound canary to a trap?
  Hide in the bushes and make a sound like birdseed.

Why do five-hundred-pound canaries wear yellow furry toe-warmers?
  To keep their toes warm.
  To lure yellow woolyworms for breakfast.

How do five-hundred-pound canaries get down chimneys?
  Hide in Santa's toy sack, then wait till Christmas.

What happened to the five-hundred-pound canary
  which landed on the beach?
  It became Sandy Claws.

If you push a six-thousand-year-old five-hundred-
  pound canary into a bowl of hot tomato soup, what
  happens?
  It drowns—five-hundred-pound canaries can't
  swim.
What did the five-hundred-pound canary say while
  walking down the street?
  Here, kitty, kitty, kitty.

How do you prevent five-hundred-pound canaries
  from charging?
  Turn off their generators.

How do you prevent five-hundred-pound canaries
  from attacking you on safaris?
  Use five-hundred-pound canary repellant.

What do five-hundred-pound canaries say when they are hungry?
CHIRP CHIRP.

Why do five-hundred-pound canaries have sharp beaks?
It makes a handy can-opener.

Why don't five-hundred-pound canaries ride bicycles?
They have enough trouble trying to ride tricycles.

Why do five-hundred-pound canaries have feathers?
Because they'd look rather silly with fur on.

What weighs five-hundred-pounds, is green, and smashes trees?
A five-hundred-pound tree frog.

What is big, lives near the beach, and wears sunglasses?
A hip five-hundred-pound seagull.

Why did the five-hundred-pound canary put its ear to the ground?
It wanted to know if a caterpillar stampede was headed its way.

Are five-hundred-pound canaries intelligent?
Of course not, they're all birdbrained.

What do five-hundred-pound canaries do on Halloween?
They go trick or tweeting.

What do five-hundred-pound canaries do on Thanksgiving?
They're glad they're not turkeys.

Why do five-hundred-pound canaries look fat?
They have poor dress designers.

When five-hundred-pound canaries fight caterpillars,
who usually loses?
The five-hundred-pound canary usually ends up
with de feet.

Why can't you trust five-hundred-pound canaries?
They're too cagey.

Why didn't the five-hundred-pound canary join the
Air Force?
It didn't need an extra set of wings.

What's the difference between a five-hundred-pound
canary and a regular canary?
Ex-Lax.

What do five-hundred-pound canaries do on Sundays?
They go to chirp.

What is large, has never been photographed, and
lives in Scotland?
The Loch Ness canary.

What do you get if you cross a road with a five-
hundred-pound canary?
Run over.

If in a restaurant you must choose between eating an
elephant egg or a five-hundred-pound canary egg,
which should you choose?
A five-hundred-pound canary egg, because everyone hates elephant yolks.

Personal Worst

Several years ago the Baltimore *Sun* published the fifty jokes which the National Association of Gagwriters had singled out as the oldest—and possibly worst—jokes of all time. Included were such classics as:

"Call me a taxi."
"Okay, you're a taxi."

and: "I just flew in from California, and my arms are tired."

The NAGW list underscores the point that some jokes are so bad that they are actually bad. Worse yet, here are some that are so bad they actually start to sound good.

Who is the first Irishman you see in the spring?
Patty O'Furniture.

Fighter: "I really want a shot at the Kid, Kid Jackson. I know I'm getting old and a little punchy, but before I retire I just want one chance in the ring with him."
Manager: "Look, if I've told you once, I've told you a hundred times. You're Kid Jackson."

Young woman to old man who has just asked her to marry. "What about sex?"
Old man: "Infrequently."
Young woman: "One word or two?"

Secretary: "Our files are so crowded that I suggest that we destroy all correspondence more than six years old."

Boss: "By all means, but be sure to make copies first."

An uncle advised his nephew: "If you can make love to a woman as long as it takes to cook a chicken, you'll be a man."

Today the nephew owns a microwave oven.

"I'm so depressed, I had to shoot my dog."

"Was he mad?"

"He wasn't exactly pleased."

An eighty-nine-year-old man and an eighty-seven-year-old woman go to an attorney's office asking for a divorce.

"This is crazy," says the lawyer. "You two have been married for over sixty years and you are getting a divorce now?"

"Look," says the husband, "we've been at each other's throat for decades now."

"Why did you wait so long?" the lawyer asks.

"Well," says the wife, "we just wanted to wait until the children were dead."

"Dad, there was a man here to see you today."

"Did he have a bill?"

"No, just an ordinary nose like yours."

Postman: "Is this package yours? The name is obliterated."

Smith: "Can't be mine, the name is Smith."

"I really loved my vacation in California," said the lady on the plane to the man sitting next to her.

"Where did you stay?" he asked.

"San Jose."

"Madam, in California we pronounce the J as H. We say San Hosay. How long were you there?"

"All of Hune and most of Huly."

"Did you hear about the fire at the shoe factory?"

"No, what happened?"

"One hundred and fifty souls were lost."

Serious Young man: "Do you enjoy Kipling?"

Young Woman: "I don't know—how do you kipple?"

"I was shot in the leg in the war."

"Have a scar?"

"No, thanks, I don't smoke."

First woman: "Why, look who's coming up the street—my husband and my boyfriend."

Second woman: "Funny, I was about to say the same thing."

Two elderly women sitting on a porch.

Q. Did you and your husband ever have mutual orgasm?

A. No, I think we had State Farm.

A drunk walks out of the Ritz Hotel, flops into a cab, and says, "Take me to the Ritz Hotel."

"We're there, sir."

"Okay," he says, throwing the driver a five-dollar bill, "but next time don't drive so fast."

Q. Where do you get your hair cut?

A. On the ends.

Q. Where is baseball mentioned in the Bible?

A. In the big inning.

Q. Why is it useless to send a message to Washington?

A. Because he's dead.

Q. What does a dog do that a man steps in?

A. Pants.

Q. What is it that a cow has four of and that a woman has two of?

A. Feet.

Q. *How can you have a Worst Joke list without at least Four (4) Good News ... Bad News Jokes?*

A. *Okay, you win—but only four!*

1. A baseball fanatic is visited by the ghost of an old teammate during the night. "Sam," says the ghost, "I've got good news—they play baseball in heaven."

"Thank God," says Sam.

"And the bad news is that they've got you starting tomorrow."

2. Galley chief to oarsman: "The good news is that you get a double ration of chow ... the bad news is that the boss wants to go water-skiing after lunch."

3. Cardinal Bernadin called all of the priests of the Chicago archdiocese to the cathedral. He said, "I've got some good news and some bad news for you. First the good news. I've talked with God and everything is okay. Now the bad news: She called from Salt Lake City."

4. Moses, coming down from the mountain with stone tablets under his arm, is greeted by an anxious multitude. "Well, friends," he says, "I have good news and bad news. I'll give you the good news first: I've got

him down to ten. Now the bad news: Adultery is still one of them."

Patient (waking up after an operation): "Why are all the shades drawn?"

Doctor: "Well, there's a fire across the street and I didn't want you think the operation was a failure."

A couple in their late seventies went to the doctor's office. The doctor asked, "What can I do for you?" The man said, "Will you watch us have sexual intercourse?" The doctor looked puzzled but agreed. When the couple had finished, the doctor said, "There is nothing wrong with the way you have intercourse." And he charged them ten dollars. This happened several weeks in a row. The couple would make an appointment, have intercourse, pay the doctor, and leave. Finally the doctor said, "Just exactly what are you trying to find out?" The old man said, "We're not trying to find out anything. She is married and we can't go to her house. I am married and we can't go to my house. Holiday Inn charges twenty-two dollars; Hilton Hotel charges twenty-seven dollars. We do it here for ten dollars and I get eight dollars back from Medicare for a visit to the doctor's office."

Why shouldn't the number 288 ever be mentioned in mixed company?

Because it's two gross.

Sam: "Call me a cab, will you?"

Joe (in uniform): "I'm not the doorman, I'm a naval officer."

Sam: "Then call me a boat."

He: "A man picked my pocket."
She: "What did he get?"
He: "Practice."

Drunk: "Taxi?"
Driver: "Yes, sir!"
Drunk: "I thought so."

What do they call an abortion in Czechoslovakia?
A canceled Czech.

What would you have if your canary got caught in your lawn mower?
Shredded Tweet!

What did Cleopatra say when Mark Antony asked if she was true to him?
Omar Khayyam.

Then there was the illegitimate Rice Krispie —snap, crackle, but no pop.

"Didn't you hear me pounding on the floor last night?"
"Oh, that's all right," replied the downstairs neighbor, "we were making a lot of noise ourselves."

A Southern woman ran up the path to the church and hurriedly asked a man, "Is Mass out?"
"No," said the man, "but your hat's on crooked."

A drunk is sitting at a bar next to a man and his wife. Suddenly he emits a tremendous belch.
"How dare you? What do you mean, belching before my wife?" demanded the man.
"Pardon me," says the drunk as he gets down off the stool, "I had no idea it was the lady's turn."

One cockroach runs into another in a drain.
"Did you hear about the new restaurant?" says one roach. "It's unbelievable—the refrigerator looks like polished silver, the shelves are clean as a whistle and—"

"Stop," says the other roach. "Not while I'm eating!"

Student: "Is this ice cream pure?"
Soda jerk: "As pure as the girl of your dreams."
Student: "Gimme a pack of cigarettes."

A man is registering at a hotel with a woman who is not his wife. He takes the pen handed to him by the room clerk and draws an X on the register. Then with a thoughtful look on his face, he circles the X.

"Lots of people sign with an X," says the clerk, "but this is the first time I've ever seen one with a circle around it."

"Nothing odd," says the man. "There are times when a person doesn't want to use his real name."

Holdup man: "Stick 'em up or else."
Victim: "Or else what?"
Holdup man: "Don't confuse me—this is my first job."

Teacher: "Where was the Declaration of Independence signed?"
Kid: "At the bottom."

He: "Would you commit adultery for a million dollars?"
She: "Why, I think I might."
He: "How about two dollars?"
She: "What do you think I am?"
He: "We've settled that. What we're haggling about is the price."

Drugstore clerk: "Did you kill any moths with those mothballs I sold you the other day?"
Customer: "No, I tried for hours and couldn't hit one."

"I know a girl who can play the piano by ear."

"That's nothing. I know a man who fiddles with his whiskers."

"I'd like a pair of stockings for my wife."
"Sheer?"
"No, she's at home."

"What is nitrate of sodium?"
"I'd imagine it's half the day rate."

Watching his new employee count out the day's receipts, the boss walked over and asked the man where he had gotten his financial training.
"Yale," he answered.
"Good. And what is your name?"
"Yackson."

Did you hear about the man whose cat got run over by a steamroller?
He didn't say anything—he just stood there with a long puss.

A man walks into a psychiatrist's office with a large hatbox. He opens it to reveal, to the doctor's shock, the head of a woman who is wearing a large flowered hat.
"This is terrible," the doctor gasps.
"Yeah," says the maniac, "that's what I told her when she paid fifty dollars for it."

What's green and red and goes a hundred miles an hour?
A frog in a blender.

"No," said the centipede, crossing her legs, "a hundred times no!"

"Send somebody over right away," said the excited

lady on the phone to the policeman. "There's an enormous gray animal in my garden pulling up cabbages with his tail."

"What's he doing?"

"If I told you," said the woman, "you'd never believe me."

If two's company, and three's a crowd, what are four and five?

Nine.

What's a metaphor?

To keep cows in.

Why do bees hum?

Because they don't know lyrics.

All the animals came on the ark in pairs—except for the worms. They came in apples.

To whom it may concern,

Please send me a copy of your most recent catalog and price list.

Most cordially,

P.S. You need not send the catalog and price list. I have changed my mind.

"How do you feel after eating all those pancakes?"

"Waffle."

We interrupt these jokes to bring back three bop jokes from the early 1950s.

1. The man walking in front of the two bopsters falls into an open manhole.

"Hey, fellows, give me a hand," he calls from underground.

"Okay," they say as they begin to applaud.

2. Two cats are finishing their meal. One says, "Think I'll have a piece of apple pie."

"Sorry," says the waitress, "but the apple pie is gone."

"Crazy, I'll take two pieces."

3. "Man, dig that ocean," said the first bopster on first seeing the Pacific.

"That's nothin', pops," said the second. "That's only the top."

"I'm a pauper."

"Congratulations. Boy or girl?"

The answer is: Chicken Teriyaki.

The question is: Who is the world's only surviving kamikaze pilot?

Why do the bees buzz?

You'd buzz, too if, someone stole your honey and nectar.

She: "I'm perfect."

He: "I'm practice."

"Papa, what's a vacuum?"

"A vacuum is a void."

"I know, Papa, but vat's the void mean?"

"Answer the door."

"Hello, door."

"Say good-night, Gracie."
"Good-night, Gracie."

"You look like Helen Green."
"I look worse in pink."

"How did I get here?" the little whisk broom de-manded.
His parents replied, "We swept together."

"I would like some alligator shoes."
"What size shoes does your alligator wear?"

Then there was the chiropodist who was walking down the street and ran into one of his patients. At first he didn't recognize her, but when she spoke he said, "Oh, hello, there—I didn't know you with your shoes on."

Jokebooks and Magazines

> *Wit and humor are the distinctive possession of all mankind, and form a vital area of literature that deserves recognition and preservation.*
>
> —Nat Schmulowitz

It may rank low in the galaxy of modern outrages, but it is, in my opinion, an outrage nonetheless: written humor in general, and jokes in particular, are held in low esteem by libraries. Therefore one of the problems which face joke collectors is that jokebooks and joke magazines are damnably difficult to find. For instance, the Library of Congress has but a pitiful handful of the joke magazines and paperback originals which were so common in America from the 1920s through the early 1960s—the Golden Age of pulp joke offerings. One is likely to find a better selection of these classics at a good flea market.

Periodicals with pep and skunk (and, of course, *laffs*) are about as common as Gutenberg Bibles at our major libraries, where librarians often have never even heard of such offerings as *Fun House, Pepper, Broadway Laughs, Jackpot, Popular Jokes, Good Humor, Laff Parade, Zowie, Romp, Jest, Army Laughs, A Laugh a Minit, Cartoons and Gags, Riot,* and *Laffing Out Loud.* Most good collections of such material are in private hands.

The only bright light is the San Francisco Public Library, which houses the Schmulowitz Collection of Wit and Humor (SCOWAH). It was originally put together by the late Nat Schmulowitz, a prominent San Francisco attorney, and now contains more than seventeen-thousand books and a huge collection of magazines and other materials. It is housed in a large, crammed room in the library and to walk through it, as I have, is to see the phenomenal assortment of material that has been published. To the joke lover, it is the Louvre, the Prado, and the Sistine Chapel all rolled into one. One's eyes and mind boggle to see two shelves of Joe Miller jokebooks (one dating back to 1743), piles of old college humor magazines, more Benchley than a person could carry, and funny stuff in Finnish, Chinese, Tshi, and Gujarati (among the titles in Gujarati: *Tunki Ane Tach Ramuljo* and, of course, *Pratham Drastive Prem*).

Schmulowitz started the collection in 1947, when he gave the Library just ninety-three books, and he spent a great deal of his spare time from then until his death in 1966 adding to the collection.* He should be an inspiration to others who believe that libraries should shelter a little more laughter.

For budding collectors, here are a few quick tips: (1) Grab up as many of the old magazines and early paperbacks as you can. For the present they are great fun. As for the future, someday the libraries will wake up and you will be able to donate them and take a $1.3 million tax deduction. (2) Don't ever pass up a copy of the old *1000 Jokes* magazine, which was published from the 1930s through 1966. Great stuff. (3) Also, don't buy that line about old jokes not being funny because of changing fashions and sensibilities. There were many jokebooks published after 1900 which are still very funny. There are of course duds, too, but even

---

*If the name rings a bell, Schmulowitz was the successful defense attorney in one of this century's most celebrated murder trials. He defended comedian Roscoe "Fatty" Arbuckle in the 1920s.

these are interesting because of the number of times you run into an ancient form of a joke which you were told in the last few weeks with the preface "I just heard a new one. . . ."

Bibliography (Sort of)

There is very few good judges of humor, and they don't agree.

—Josh Billings

In putting this collection together, I read or looked at hundreds of jokebooks ranging in quality from the outstanding to the dismal. Listed bibliographically with occasional notes are those which I liked best and which could serve as a guide to anyone building up a collection. Of course, this is one man's opinion and you may not agree.

Adams, Joey. *From Gags to Riches*. New York: Frederick Fell Inc., 1946.

Adams, Joey. *Joey Adams Joke Book*. New York: Frederick Fell Inc., 1952.

Adams, Joey. *Joey Adams Joke Dictionary*. New York: Citadel, 1962.

(All these are treasure troves, especially the last one listed.)

Adler, Larry. *Jokes and How to Tell Them*. Garden City: Doubleday, 1963.

(The unusual book which really does tell you how to deliver a joke. The examples he uses are first-rate.)

Asimov, Isaac. *Treasury of Humor*. Boston: Houghton Mifflin Company, 1971.

(A smashingly good collection which everyone interested in jokes should have.)

Blake, Robert. *101 Elephant Jokes*, New York: Pyramid Books, 1964.

(You've got to have one of these and this one is the best of the elephant lot.)

Boone, Charlie, and Roger Erickson. *The Worst of Boone and Erickson*. Minneapolis: WCCO Radio, 1977.

Cagney, Peter. *Treasury of Wit and Humor*. Preston: A. Thomas and Co., 1965.

Carlinsky, Dan. *A Century of College Humor*. New York: Random House, 1971.

Cerf, Bennett. All of his joke collections, which number fifteen. All of them are good, although some jokes show up in more than one book. I can't imagine anyone interested in jokes not having a bunch of these books.

Clark, David Allen. *Jokes, Puns and Riddles*. New York: Doubleday, 1968.

Coggins, Herbert L. *Knick Knacks*. Philadelphia: Penn Publishing Co., 1906.

Cohen, Myron. *The Myron Cohen Joke Book*. New York: Gramercy, 1978.

Copeland, Lewis. *The World's Best Jokes*. New York: Halcyon House, 1936.

Croy, Homer. *What Grandpa Laughed At*. New York: Duell, Sloan and Pearce, 1948.

David McKay Publisher. *A Thousand and One Riddles with a Few Thrown In*. Philadelphia: no date.

Davis, J. J. *The Entomologists' Jokebook*. Exterminator's Log. Lafayette, Ind., 1937.

Esar, Evan. *Esar's Comic Dictionary*. New York: Harvest House, 1943.

Esar, Evan. *The Humor of Humor*. New York: Bramhall House, 1952.

Fadiman, Clifton. *Any Number Can Play*. Cleveland: World, 1957.

(Especially important for Fadiman's essay on punning.)

Fechtner, Leopold. *Encyclopedia of Ad-Libs, Insults and Wisecracks*. West Nyack, N.Y.: Parker Publishing Co., 1977.

Fechtner, Leopold. *5,000 One and Two Liners for Any and Every Occasion*. West Nyack, N.Y.: Parker Publishing Co., 1973.

Fredericks, Vic. *Crackers in Bed*. New York: Pocket Books, 1953.

Gigem Press. *The Best of 606 Aggie Jokes*. Dallas: 1976.

Hample, Stoo. *Silly Joke Book*. New York: Delacorte Press, 1978.

Hart, Harold. *Top Stuff*. New York: Parker Press, 1945.

Hershfield, Harry. *The Harry Hershfield Joke Book*. New York: Ballantine Books, 1964.

Hershfield, Harry. *Laugh Louder, Live Longer*. New York: Grayson Publishing Co., 1959.

Hershfield, Harry. *Now I'll Tell One*. New York: Greenberg, 1938.

Keller, Charles. *Laughing*. Englewood Cliffs, N.J.: Prentice-Hall, Inc., 1977.

Keseling, Peter C. and John Kinney. *Summa Cum Laughter*. New York: Waldorf Publishing Corp., 1956.

Kopper, Richard, Richard Irvine, and John Burns. *A Treasury of College Humor*. New York: William Penn Publishing Co., 1950.

Lake, Anthony B. *A Pleasury of Witticisms and Word Play*. New York: Bramhall, 1965.

Lauber, Patricia. *Jokes and More Jokes*. New York: Scholastic Book Services, 1967.

Leeming, Joseph. *Riddles, Riddles, Riddles*. New York: Franklin Watts, Inc., 1953.

Levinson, Leonard. *Webster's Unafraid Dictionary*. New York: Macmillan, 1967.

Lieberman, Jerry. *Off the Cuff*. New York: Pocket Books, 1956.

Moger, Art. *The Complete Pun Book*. Secaucus, N.J.: The Citadel Press, 1979.

Moulten, Powers. *2500 Jokes*. New York: New Home Library, 1942.

Murray, Ken. *Giant Joke Book*. New York: Ace Books, 1954.

Orben, Robert. All of his titles. (Orben is the king

of one-line comedy and he has lines for every subject under the sun. Especially recommended is *2100 Laughs for All Occasions,* Doubleday, 1982.)

Partridge, Eric. *The Shaggy Dog Story.* New York: Philosophical Library, 1954.

Price/Stern/Sloan publishers. *The Elephant Book.* Los Angeles: 1972.

Ripley, Elizabeth. *Lots of Laughs.* New York: Oxford University Press, 1942.

Schwartz, Alvin. *Tomfoolery.* Philadelphia: J. B. Lippincott, 1973.

Shulman, Max. *Guided Tour of Campus Humor.* Garden City: Hanover House, 1955.

Smith, H. Allen. *Buskin' with H. Allen Smith.* New York: Pocket Books, 1969.

Tolliver, Bernard, P. *Barrel of Laughs.* New York: Hart Publishing Co., 1960.

Untermeyer, Louis. *A Treasury of Laughter.* New York: Simon and Schuster, 1946.

Wachs, Mark. *The Funniest Jokes and How to Tell Them.* New York: Hawthorne, 1968.

Wells, Carolyn. *Such Nonsense.* New York: George H. Doran Co., 1918.

Wilde, Larry. All of his titles. Wilde is the most prolific of modern jokebook writers and each of his books covers a subject from A to Z. To date he has covered most of the major ethnic targets.

Winick, Charles. *Outer Space Humor.* Mount Vernon, N.Y.: Peter Pauper Press, 1963.

Wright, Milton. *What's Funny and Why.* New York: Harvest House, 1953.

Yates, Bill. *Laughing on the Inside.* New York: Dell Publishing Co., 1953.

Youngman, Henny. All of his titles. Take them all . . . please!

Joke Museum Announced

It occurred to me as I finished this book that it would be a good idea to start a joke museum as a central repository for the oddments of jokedom. It would have wings dedicated to joke superstars—psychiatrists, mothers-in-law, absentminded professors, drunks, Scotchmen—and would work to preserve endangered joke species, as in "There was this traveling salesman . . ." It would collect and display the true museum pieces: presidential puns, the oldest jokes, the shortest jokes, notorious jokes (such as those which got politicians in trouble for telling them), and more.

Plans are still a bit sketchy, but it would have to have a great hall of puns where all the great pun punch lines would be on display and there would have to be a philosophy division where you could visit all those great "Confucius say . . ." lines like, "Many men smoke, but Fu Manchu," "Wash face in morning. Neck at night," and "Husband who know where wife keep nickels has nothing on one who know where maid's quarters are."

A few other ideas for collections and displays within the museum:

Fad Jokes. For instance, the 3-D movie craze of the 1950s left such gems as these: Hollywood is now working on a 3-D film that if you don't go into the theater to see it, it comes out to see you. . . . Man at 3-D movie: "Lady, would you please remove your hat, I can't see." Lady: "I'm sorry, sir, it's part of the movie." . . . The Pentagon has just completed a movie made in

9-D, that's 3-D in triplicate. . . . "Baby, you'd look great in 3-D," said the producer to the starlet. "Would it be in Technicolor?" she responded. "No," said the producer, "that's my hotel-room number."

Multiple Puns. It has been claimed that this is as perfect a triple pun as the language offers. A woman's three sons go to Texas to raise cattle, hogs, and sheep. After a while they write to her and say that all is fine except for the fact that they have been unable to come up with a name for the ranch.

"NAME IT FOCUS," she telegraphed.

The boys were puzzled and cabled back for an explanation.

Her reply: "FOCUS—WHERE THE SUN'S RAYS MEET."

Show me's, as in "Show me a careless owl and I'll show you a bird that doesn't give a hoot."

Or's, as in Or, as the fly said as he walked up the mirror, "That's another way of looking at it," Or, as Lady Godiva said at the end of her famous ride, "I am drawing near to my close," Or, as the ram said as he plunged off the cliff, "I didn't see that ewe turn," and, Or, as the scientist said just after he had cloned himself, "I'm beside myself with happiness."

Inanimate object jokes, such as the one can of paint which says to the other can of paint, "Darling, I think I'm pigment."

Anyone who would like to suggest ideas for the museum or contribute jokes can write to the author care of: Joke Museum, Box 80, Garrett Park, Maryland 20896.

But Seriously, Folks . . .

Small groups of persons without a sense of humor can do as much damage to America as small groups of communists in high places.
> —William F. Treadwell
> before meeting the
> American Public
> Relations Society,
> February 21, 1955.

I am deeply indebted to a number of people for their help collecting the jokes needed for this book. Together they make up the counterforce to those knots of humorless subversives capable of doing so much damage to the Republic.

Bob Ackley
Don Addis
Nancy Alden
Reinhold Aman
W. R. Anderson
Joseph E. Badger
Kent Bailey
Mike Baldwin
Karen Marie Bartol
David F. Berger
Charlie Boon
Caroline Bryan
Samuel Cabot

Shel Kagan
Ron Kaye
Martin S. Kottmeyer
Norbert Kraich
Mary Kramer
Alan G. Lewis
David S. Little
Kenneth B. Livingston
Mel Loftus
Dale Lowdermilk
Neil Harding McAlister,
    M.D.
Cynthia MacGregor

C. H. Channing
John Clark
William Cole
Glenn Collins
Maureen Connolly
Charles Conrard III
Paul W. Corchran, M.D.
Martha Cornog
Don Crinklaw
Clifford Crist
S. Percy Dean
John R. DeMonte
Al deQuoy
Arthur J. Deex
C. Henry Depew
Tom Dial
Nancy Dickson
Russell J. Dunn, Sr.
T. S. Durham
Pat H. Everett
John D. Fitzgerald
Steve Fried
Joel Garreau
Walt Giachini
James G. Gillivan
Jeffrey H. Goldstein
Joel Goodman
Rev. Frederick G.
  Gotwald
Joseph C. Goulden
Fr. Don Graff
Marvin Grosswirth
Steven Haase
Irving Hale
Arnold Harris
N. Sally Hass
John M. Hazlitt
George A. Heinemann

Norman Mark
Steve Masse
Charles Mintzlaff
Paul Mouchon
Leslie Nelson
Bob Orben
Charles L. Orr
Dennis Panke
J. Beauregard Pepys
Timothy Perper
Irene H. Phillippe
Tom Quantance
Suzie Radus
Mark Rausch
Harvey Roehl
William A. Rooney
Cornelius Van S.
  Roosevelt
Jim Rubins
William Safire
Lauren Barnett Scharf
Penny Scott and her
  students
John Seiffer
Robert W. Sellen
Johnathan S. Silber
Bob Skole
Robert Smith
Richard C. Smolik
R. C. Snider
George R. Soika
John A. Staedler
Ashley Steele
Jeff Strickler
William Tammeus
Mike Thaler
John G. Thompson
Robert J. Throckmorton

Thanks again, or, as the woman said to her urologist husband, "Having you around makes a vas deferens."